Fact Mastery
Addition & Subtraction

Improve Automaticity and Accuracy of Basic Facts with Thinking Strategies, Sequential Practice Pages, Easy-to-Play Partner Games, and Timed Tests

by
Debra O. Pressnall

illustrated by
Vanessa Countryman

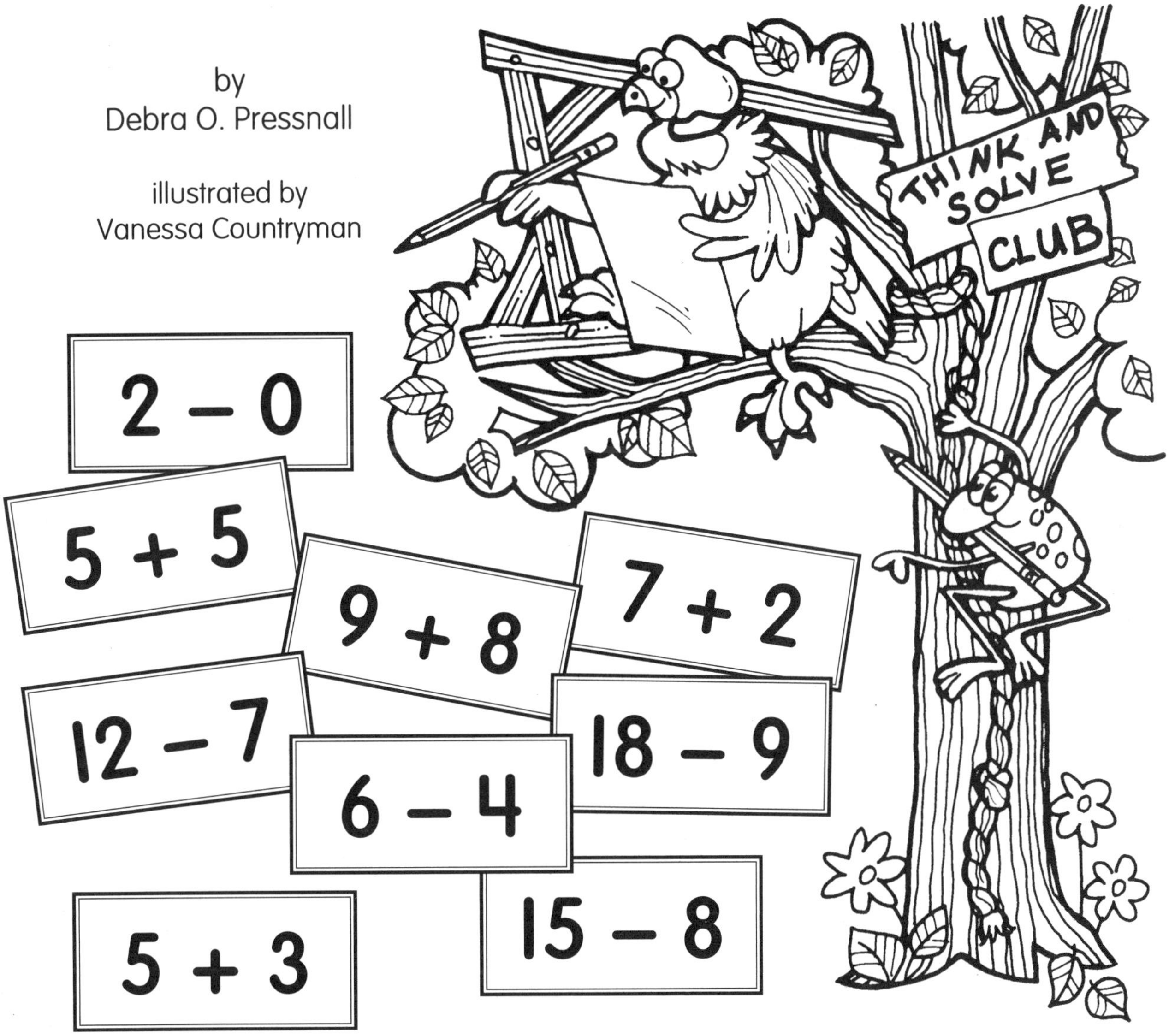

Publisher
Key Education Publishing Company, LLC
Minneapolis, Minnesota

www.keyeducationpublishing.com

CONGRATULATIONS ON YOUR PURCHASE OF A KEY EDUCATION PRODUCT!

The editors at Key Education are former teachers who bring experience, enthusiasm, and quality to each and every product. Thousands of teachers have looked to the staff at Key Education for new and innovative resources to make their work more enjoyable and rewarding. We are committed to developing educational materials that will assist teachers in building a strong and developmentally appropriate curriculum for young children.

PLAN FOR GREAT TEACHING EXPERIENCES WHEN YOU USE EDUCATIONAL MATERIALS FROM KEY EDUCATION PUBLISHING COMPANY, LLC

Credits
Author: Debra O. Pressnall
Publisher: Sherrill B. Flora
Illustrator: Vanessa Countryman
Editors: Debra Pressnall and Karen Seberg
Cover Design and Production: Annette Hollister-Papp
Page Layout: Key Education Staff
Cover Photograph: © Digital Vision

Key Education welcomes manuscripts and product ideas from teachers. For a copy of our submission guidelines, send a self-addressed, stamped envelope to:

Key Education Publishing Company, LLC
Acquisitions Department
9601 Newton Avenue South
Minneapolis, Minnesota 55431

Standard Book Number: 978-1-602680-48-7
Fact Mastery: Addition & Subtraction

Minneapolis, Minnesota 55431

Table of Contents

Fact Mastery: Sums 11 to 20

Sums 11 to 20—Missing Addend

Fact Mastery: Minuends 11 to 20

Other Resources

Introduction

The ability to recall answers for basic math facts quickly and accurately is an important and necessary skill for children as they acquire mathematical knowledge that will later support the learning of algebra. In March 2008, the National Mathematics Advisory Panel released its findings *Foundations for Success: The Final Report of the National Mathematics Advisory Panel* (U.S. Department of Education, Washington, DC). Regarding the commitment of math facts to long-term memory, the Panel stated "computational facility with whole number operations rests on the automatic recall of addition and related subtraction facts, and of multiplication and related division facts." *Fact Mastery: Addition & Subtraction* provides the tools to help children reach this level of mastery recommended by the National Mathematics Advisory Panel.

Fact Mastery: Addition & Subtraction also supports the NCTM (National Council of Teachers of Mathematics) Standards and *Curriculum Focal Points for Prekindergarten through Grade 8 Mathematics* (2006) by offering materials that help students acquire strategies for learning the facts and understanding them. To achieve this goal, this resource book targets essential skill development by introducing addition and subtraction facts in a systematic manner and by providing specific activities for practicing them.

How to Use This Book

Listed below are a few suggestions for ways to use the reproducible materials provided in this resource book.

- **Using pretest/posttest assessment tools.** In each section of this book, you will find an assessment test, 49 problems in length, that can be completed during a predetermined amount of time or without a time constraint. Use each assessment test to identify which facts the student needs to master.

- **Introducing and using mental strategies to learn basic facts.** To help students acquire a greater understanding of numbers and relationships between numbers, it is recommended that students learn how to use mental strategies when memorizing the basic facts. Throughout the book, you will find pages for practicing various thinking strategies. The Show and Solve pages as well as the Think and Solve pages can be used as tools to introduce specific strategies and math facts. Additional information about the recommended strategies is provided on the introductory page for each section of the book. As new math facts are introduced, you might consider having students print them on index cards to make personal sets of flash cards.

- **Using the Fast Fact practice pages.** These half-page exercises can be used as warm-up activities during math class or by students who need additional practice before they are ready to take the Quick Check or 50 Nifty Facts timed tests. If necessary, have students complete the Fast Fact pages by alternating between top and bottom halves until they achieve mastery.

- **Setting up your math center and using the 15 easy-to-play partner games.** When making the math games, be sure to cut out and glue a copy of the game directions to the back of each game board for a quick reference. Store the materials in large zippered plastic bags. After specific mental strategies and facts have been introduced, use the partner games as a motivating tool to help students learn those facts.

- **Using the Quick Check and 50 Nifty Facts timed tests.** The Quick Checks are 36 problems in length and it is recommended that you allow students *two minutes* to complete each one. For each 50 Nifty Facts exercise, allow students *three minutes* to answer the problems. Depending on the capabilities of your students, predetermine the percentage of accuracy each student must achieve before moving on to another set of tests. If you are using the 50 Nifty Facts pages, alternate between tests A and B until students achieve the desired proficiency. Check off the tests as students complete them on a copy of the corresponding Progress Chart.

Fact Mastery: Sums to 10

Helping students learn and apply different strategies when memorizing the sums of basic addition facts is an important step. As each strategy is introduced, print its name in a prominent location. Then, students may refer to the list when solving math problems on the Show and Solve, Think and Solve, and Fast Facts practice pages. *To help students develop the habit of using mental strategies, it is recommended that they verbalize their methods for solving the math problems to their partners.* Point out how it is possible to calculate the answer for a problem in different ways.

Strategies to Introduce and Use

Count On (+0, +1, +2). When students are adding two numbers together, have them look for the addend 0, 1, or 2 and then use that number to count on from a larger addend. Eventually, students need to internalize these sums and not depend on counting on their fingers or objects. Pair off students and have them tell each other the sums of addition problems that you call out. Use the facts introduced on pages 9 and 10.

Switch the Order of Addends. Not all problems will list the larger addend first. Help students learn to recognize when it is necessary to switch the order of the addends to solve the problems. Pair off students. Call out math facts and have students tell each other the larger addend and restate the math problem, if necessary, so that the larger number is mentioned first. Use the facts introduced on pages 12 and 14.

Doubles, Doubles. When students know the double facts, it is easy for them to apply that knowledge to solve other basic addition problems. To help students visualize the concept of doubles, you might consider using models for the double facts. For example, a little red wagon has two wheels on each side for 2 + 2. A picture of an insect's legs would demonstrate 3 + 3. Two large dice arranged side by side can be used to show 4 + 4 or 5 + 5. Have students write the double facts on index cards for additional practice. Use the facts introduced on page 20.

Doubles Less 1. For this strategy, direct students to double the first addend of the given problem to make the double fact and then compare the problems. For example, if 4 + 4 = 8, then the sum for 4 + 3 will be 1 less than 8, which is 7. Have students pair off and solve the problems that you call out. Use the facts introduced on page 20. You might also have students write those facts on index cards for additional practice.

Doubles Plus 1. For this strategy, direct students to make the double fact and then compare the addends. For example, if 4 + 4 = 8, then the sum for 4 + 5 will be 1 more than 8, which is 9. Have students pair off and solve the problems that you call out. Use the facts introduced on page 21. Students may write those facts on index cards for additional drill.

Sums of 10. Once students know the combinations of addends that equal the sum of 10, they can use those facts to solve other math problems. Have students write those facts on index cards for additional drill. Be sure to include both related facts on the same card. For example, 7 + 3 and 3 + 7 would be printed on the front of a card. Have students work in pairs to learn these facts. This set of facts includes 5 + 5 (on pages 20 and 27) and 6 + 4 and 7 + 3 (on page 29). The facts 8 + 2 and 9 + 1 are featured with the "Count On" strategy.

Special Facts. For some facts, there are not clear strategies that can be used to solve them. Sometimes, it is helpful to compare those facts to the double facts (on page 27) and sums of 10 facts (on page 29). Direct students to write those facts on index cards and practice them frequently. Be sure to include both related facts on the same card. For example: 6 + 3 and 3 + 6 would be printed on the front of a card. The addition problems 5 + 3 and 6 + 3 (on page 27) are treated as special facts. Have students work in pairs to learn these facts while reviewing other facts.

How Far Apart? Choose a Strategy. When working with missing addends, students need to think about how far the given addend is from the sum before choosing a strategy to solve the problem. Are those numbers "next door neighbors"? If *yes,* students can then use the "Count Up" strategy. If not, they could use the "Count Back" strategy. For example, to solve 4 + _ = 10, students can count back 4 numbers from 10 to determine that the missing addend is 6. Another strategy would be to double the given addend and then compare numbers. For example, to solve 4 + _ = 10, think 4 + 4 = 8 and then determine that the missing addend needs to be 2 more than 4, or 6, to make the sum of 10. Have students pair off for the mental math activities. Call out various missing addend problems for them to discuss and solve. Use the problems listed on pages 37, 39, 41, 44, and 46.

Name ______________________ Date ______________

Pretest/Posttest

Score: ________

A	7 + 2	1 + 1	5 + 3	9 + 1	4 + 6	2 + 4	3 + 1
B	6 + 2	8 + 0	3 + 4	2 + 8	4 + 4	1 + 4	2 + 3
C	5 + 5	2 + 1	6 + 2	3 + 5	0 + 6	5 + 2	1 + 9
D	2 + 7	4 + 5	3 + 6	3 + 3	9 + 0	7 + 3	4 + 1
E	3 + 0	2 + 5	5 + 1	6 + 3	7 + 1	1 + 8	4 + 2
F	2 + 2	3 + 7	8 + 2	0 + 5	1 + 7	4 + 0	6 + 4
G	5 + 4	6 + 1	7 + 0	2 + 6	4 + 3	1 + 3	3 + 2

Progress Chart

Sums to 10

Name	Quick Check A	Quick Check B	Quick Check C	Quick Check D	Quick Check E	Quick Check F	50 Facts A	50 Facts B

Show and Solve

Thinking Strategy:
Count On (+0, +1)

1 Show the problem.

+

2 Think of the answer.

3 Show the sum.

Directions Use math counters to solve each problem. Write the sum in the blank.

1 + 0 = ___	8 + 0 = ___	2 + 1 = ___	9 + 0 = ___	5 + 1 = ___
7 + 1 = ___	3 + 1 = ___	6 + 0 = ___	2 + 0 = ___	4 + 1 = ___

Show and Solve

Thinking Strategy:
Count On (+1, +2)

1 Show the problem.

+

2 Think of the answer.

3 Show the sum.

Directions Use math counters to solve each problem. Write the sum in the blank.

3 + 2 = ___ 7 + 2 = ___ 1 + 1 = ___ 4 + 2 = ___ 8 + 1 = ___

5 + 2 = ___ 6 + 1 = ___ 8 + 2 = ___ 9 + 1 = ___ 6 + 2 = ___

Name ______________________ Date ______________

Fast Facts 1

Sums to 10

The activity coordinates with pages 9 and 10.

3 + 0 = ___

6 + 0 = ___

6 + 1 = ___

3 + 2 = ___

5 + 0 = ___

2 + 2 = ___

7 + 2 = ___

8 + 2 = ___

4 + 1 = ___

5 + 1 = ___

5 + 2 = ___

8 + 0 = ___

Name ______________________ Date ______________

Fast Facts 2

Sums to 10

The activity coordinates with pages 9 and 10.

7 + 0 = ___

1 + 2 = ___

4 + 2 = ___

3 + 1 = ___

9 + 1 = ___

6 + 2 = ___

4 + 0 = ___

2 + 2 = ___

9 + 0 = ___

8 + 1 = ___

8 + 2 = ___

7 + 1 = ___

Name ____________ Date ____________

Show and Solve

Thinking Stategies: Switch the Order and Count On

1 Show the problem.

+

2 Think of the answer.

3 Show the sum.

Directions Use math counters to solve each problem. Circle the larger number. Write the sum in the blank.

1 + 4 = ____ 1 + 9 = ____ 2 + 4 = ____ 1 + 3 = ____ 1 + 8 = ____

2 + 5 = ____ 2 + 6 = ____ 0 + 2 = ____ 2 + 8 = ____ 2 + 7 = ____

Name ______________________ Date ____________

Fast Facts 3

Sums to 10

The activity coordinates with page 12.

$1 + 7 =$ ___

$1 + 3 =$ ___

$0 + 7 =$ ___

$0 + 5 =$ ___

$2 + 8 =$ ___

$1 + 4 =$ ___

$1 + 9 =$ ___

$0 + 6 =$ ___

$1 + 8 =$ ___

$1 + 2 =$ ___

$2 + 6 =$ ___

$2 + 4 =$ ___

Name ______________________ Date ____________

Fast Facts 4

Sums to 10

The activity coordinates with page 12.

$0 + 4 =$ ___

$0 + 3 =$ ___

$1 + 6 =$ ___

$0 + 9 =$ ___

$2 + 8 =$ ___

$2 + 5 =$ ___

$1 + 3 =$ ___

$1 + 5 =$ ___

$0 + 8 =$ ___

$2 + 7 =$ ___

$2 + 3 =$ ___

$1 + 4 =$ ___

Name ____________________ Date ____________________

Think and Solve

Thinking Strategies: Switch the Order and Count On

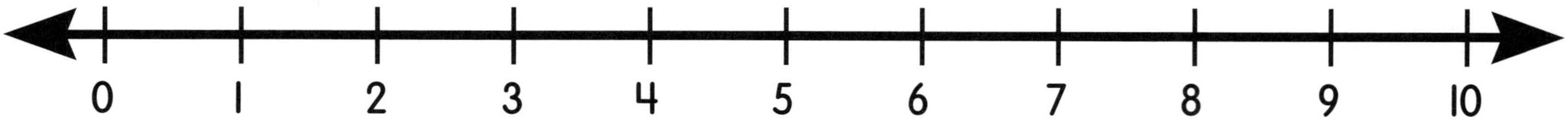

Fold on line.

Directions

- Hide the number line by folding over the top of this paper.
- Read each problem. Circle the larger number and then add.
- Write the sum in the blank.
- Use the number line to check your answers.

$2 + 3 =$ ___	$2 + 7 =$ ___	$1 + 5 =$ ___	$4 + 2 =$ ___	$1 + 8 =$ ___
$1 + 7 =$ ___	$9 + 0 =$ ___	$2 + 5 =$ ___	$2 + 4 =$ ___	$6 + 2 =$ ___
$2 + 6 =$ ___	$8 + 1 =$ ___	$1 + 6 =$ ___	$3 + 2 =$ ___	$0 + 8 =$ ___
$1 + 4 =$ ___	$2 + 8 =$ ___	$1 + 9 =$ ___	$5 + 2 =$ ___	$7 + 2 =$ ___

Name ____________________ Date ____________

Fast Facts 5

Sums to 10

The activity coordinates with page 14.

2 + 7 = ___ 2 + 4 = ___

3 + 2 = ___ 1 + 9 = ___

0 + 3 = ___ 5 + 2 = ___

5 + 1 = ___ 0 + 2 = ___ 0 + 5 = ___

1 + 3 = ___ 4 + 1 = ___ 6 + 1 = ___

Name ____________________ Date ____________

Fast Facts 6

Sums to 10

The activity coordinates with page 14.

2 + 8 = ___ 6 + 2 = ___

5 + 0 = ___ 3 + 1 = ___

4 + 0 = ___ 0 + 8 = ___

7 + 1 = ___ 2 + 5 = ___ 4 + 2 = ___

1 + 6 = ___ 9 + 1 = ___ 2 + 3 = ___

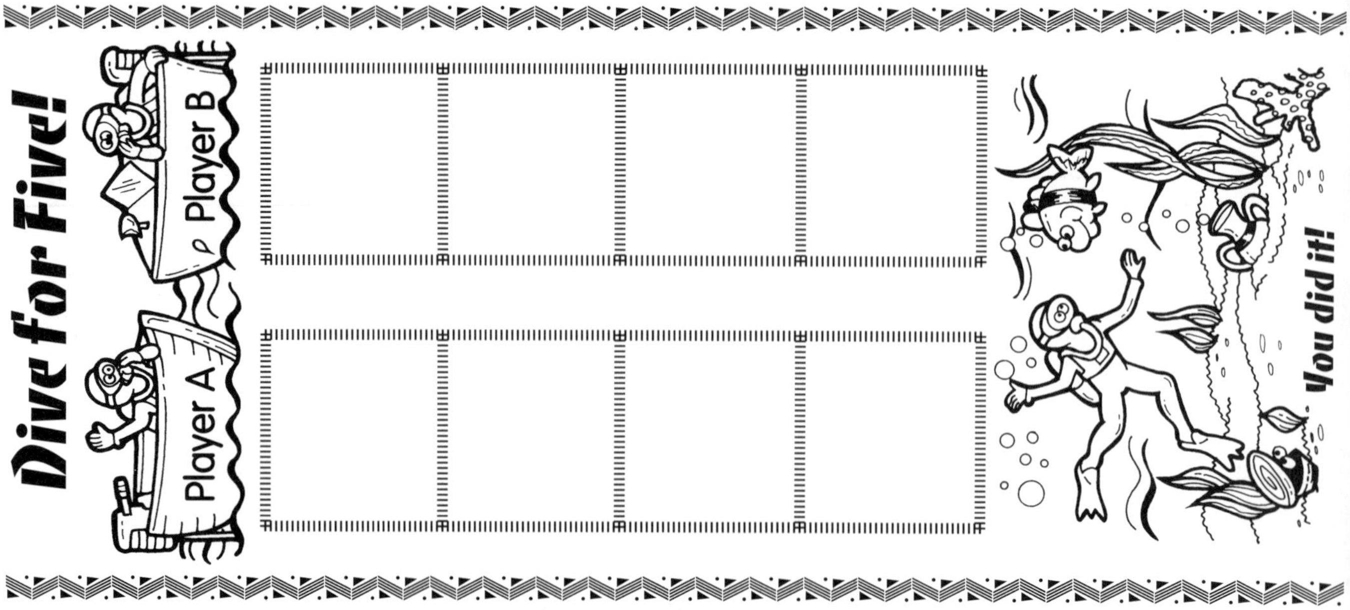

Partner Game—Dive for Five!

Getting Ready: Copy this page and the numeral cards on page 17 onto colorful card stock. Cut out the game pieces along the dashed lines. To form the die, fold along the solid lines to make the cube shape and then glue the tabs as indicated under the numerals. Tape the edges of the cube for durability. Provide two game markers.

Playing the Game: Scatter the numeral cards facedown in the center of the playing area. Player A places a game marker on the boat, rolls the die, and then draws one game card. When the card is turned faceup, the player must add the number shown on the die to the game card and *say the addition sentence out loud.* Player B should listen carefully for errors. If the answer is correct, Player A moves the game marker down to the first box on the game board. If the answer is incorrect, Player A may not move the game marker. Player B takes a turn and continues the game in the same manner. If the words "Go back to the boat!" are rolled, the player must move the game marker back to the boat. All of the numeral cards are returned facedown to the playing area whenever they are needed. The game ends when one or both players reach the bottom of the sea.

Addend Die

+1

Glue here.

+0

+2

Go back to the boat!

+2

Glue here.

Glue here.

+1

4

8

3

8

2

7

1

6

0

5

Name ______________________ Date ______________

Quick Check A

Sums to 10

The test is on facts from pages 9–15. Alternate it with Quick Check B.

Score: ________

Time:

A	1 + 9	5 + 1	0 + 6	1 + 8	1 + 2	8 + 2
B	0 + 10	1 + 7	2 + 5	0 + 2	4 + 2	6 + 1
C	1 + 3	3 + 2	8 + 0	2 + 6	3 + 0	7 + 1
D	2 + 7	4 + 1	8 + 1	0 + 7	1 + 4	5 + 2
E	0 + 1	2 + 4	1 + 5	7 + 2	2 + 1	9 + 1
F	2 + 3	3 + 1	0 + 9	2 + 8	1 + 6	6 + 2

Name ______________________ Date ______________

Quick Check B

Sums to 10

The test is on facts from pages 9–15. Alternate it with Quick Check A.

Score: ________

Time:

A	6 + 2	1 + 9	0 + 4	2 + 4	1 + 4	7 + 1
B	9 + 1	8 + 2	1 + 7	5 + 1	9 + 0	2 + 6
C	2 + 3	1 + 3	4 + 2	8 + 1	2 + 8	4 + 1
D	2 + 7	0 + 3	1 + 5	7 + 0	3 + 2	2 + 1
E	2 + 5	3 + 1	7 + 2	1 + 2	6 + 1	0 + 9
F	1 + 1	1 + 8	10 + 0	1 + 6	4 + 0	5 + 2

Show and Solve

Thinking Strategies: Doubles and Doubles Less 1

1 Show the problem.

+

2 Think of the answer.

3 Show the sum.

Directions

Use math counters to solve each problem. If the math fact is not a double, tell your partner the double that is closest to it. Write the sum in the blank.

5 + 5 = ___ 2 + 2 = ___ 5 + 4 = ___ 1 + 0 = ___ 1 + 1 = ___

2 + 1 = ___ 3 + 3 = ___ 3 + 2 = ___ 4 + 4 = ___ 4 + 3 = ___

Name ____________ Date ____________

Show and Solve

1 Show the problem.

+

2 Think of the answer.

3 Show the sum.

Directions

Use math counters to solve each problem. If the math fact is not a double, tell your partner the double that is closest to it. Write the sum in the blank.

4 + 4 = ___ 1 + 1 = ___ 3 + 4 = ___ 1 + 2 = ___ 0 + 0 = ___

4 + 5 = ___ 3 + 3 = ___ 2 + 2 = ___ 0 + 1 = ___ 2 + 3 = ___

Name ______________________ Date ______________

Fast Facts 7

Sums to 10

The activity coordinates with pages 20 and 21.

5 + 5 = ___

3 + 4 = ___

2 + 1 = ___

2 + 3 = ___

4 + 5 = ___

4 + 4 = ___

4 + 3 = ___

3 + 2 = ___

2 + 2 = ___

1 + 1 = ___

5 + 4 = ___

3 + 3 = ___

Name ______________________ Date ______________

Fast Facts 8

Sums to 10

The activity coordinates with pages 20 and 21.

3 + 4 = ___

5 + 5 = ___

2 + 1 = ___

2 + 3 = ___

4 + 3 = ___

4 + 4 = ___

1 + 2 = ___

5 + 4 = ___

0 + 0 = ___

3 + 3 = ___

3 + 2 = ___

4 + 5 = ___

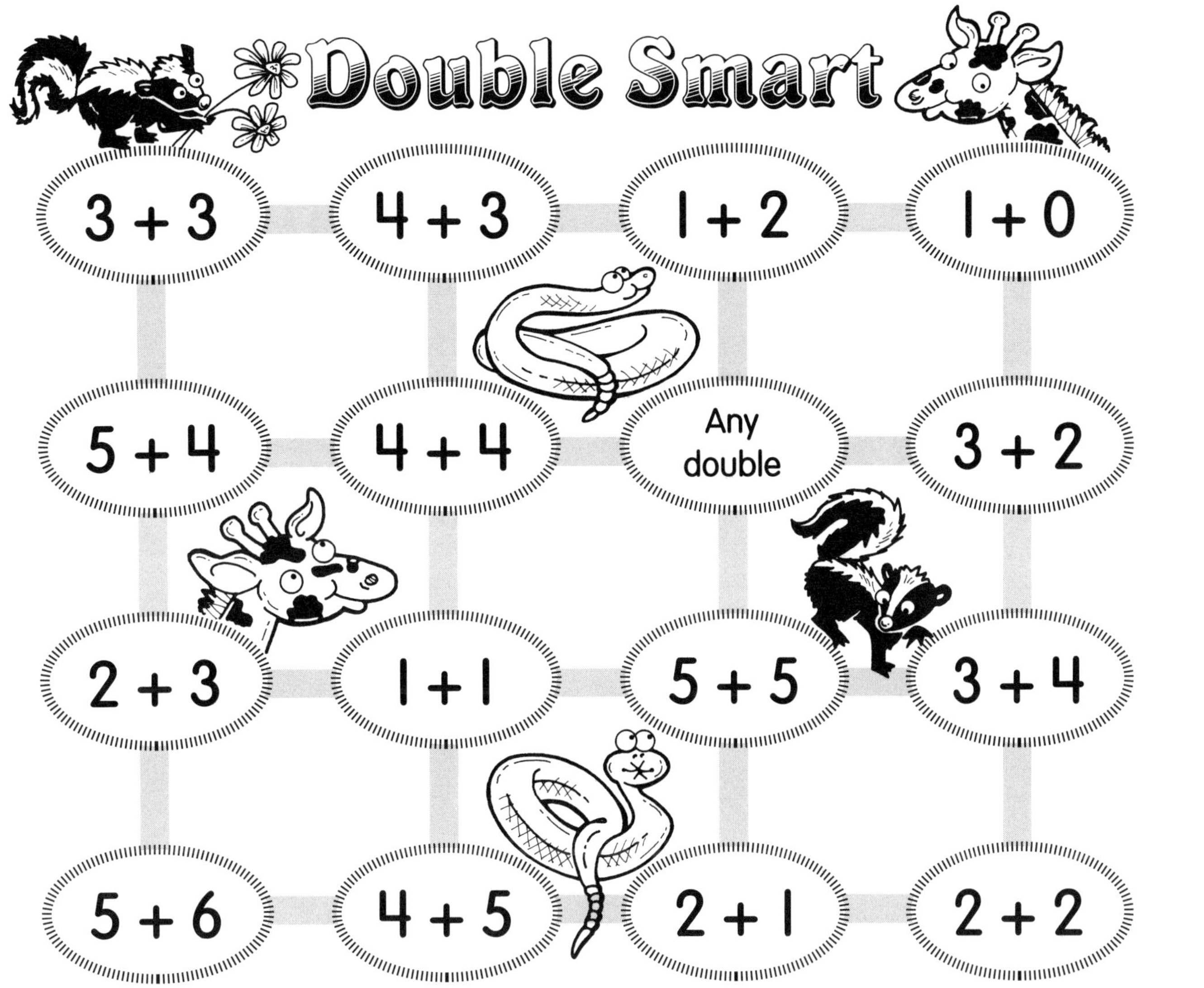

Partner Game—Double Smart

Getting Ready: Copy the game board on this page and the dice on page 24 onto colorful card stock. Cut out the game pieces along the dashed lines. To form each die, fold along the solid lines to make the cube shape and then glue the tabs as indicated under the numerals. Provide 10 identical game markers for each player.

Playing the Game: Give each player a set of game markers. Place the game board in the center of the playing area. To begin the game, Player A rolls the dice and adds the numbers together. The player must say the math sentence correctly out loud and then look for the corresponding problem on the game board. Player B should listen carefully to catch any errors. For example, if 3 + 3 and + 1 are rolled, Player A says, "3 + 3 + 1 is the same as 3 + 4." Player A covers the correct fact (3 + 4) on the game board. (The first number in the fact establishes the double for comparison.) If the fact has already been covered or if Player A does not verbalize the math sentence correctly, Player A's turn is over. Player B then takes a turn. If the words "Any double" are rolled, the player chooses which double to use to make the math fact. To cover the words "Any double" on the game board, the player must roll a double and + 0. The game ends when one player covers four spaces in a vertical, horizontal, or diagonal row. Otherwise, the player who covers the most spaces wins the game.

Doubles Die

Glue here.

5 + 5 | 1 + 1 | 3 + 3 | Any double | Glue here.

4 + 4

Glue here.

2 + 2

Addend Die

Glue here.

+0 | −1 | +0 | −1 | Glue here.

+1

Glue here.

+1

Name ______________________ Date ______________

Quick Check C

Sums to 10

The test is on facts from pages 20–22 and previously learned facts. Alternate it with Quick Check D. The new facts are repeated for extra practice.

Score: ________

Time:

A	2 + 4	3 + 2	9 + 1	1 + 2	7 + 2	5 + 5
B	4 + 4	2 + 7	4 + 5	3 + 4	1 + 1	3 + 3
C	4 + 2	5 + 4	3 + 1	6 + 2	2 + 3	4 + 3
D	0 + 0	8 + 2	3 + 4	5 + 5	7 + 1	2 + 5
E	5 + 2	3 + 3	2 + 6	4 + 5	1 + 8	2 + 1
F	2 + 2	5 + 4	4 + 4	5 + 1	4 + 3	2 + 8

Name ______________________ Date ______________

Quick Check D

Sums to 10

The test is on facts from pages 20–22 and previously learned facts.
Alternate it with Quick Check C. The new facts are repeated for extra practice.

Score: ____________

Time:

A	6 + 2	5 + 4	1 + 9	2 + 3	6 + 1	3 + 4
B	4 + 5	5 + 1	5 + 5	7 + 2	4 + 3	1 + 1
C	1 + 0	3 + 3	8 + 2	2 + 2	4 + 2	4 + 4
D	5 + 5	10 + 0	3 + 2	2 + 6	3 + 4	4 + 1
E	5 + 2	4 + 4	8 + 1	5 + 4	2 + 4	1 + 2
F	4 + 3	2 + 7	3 + 3	6 + 0	2 + 1	4 + 5

Name ______________________ Date ______________

Show and Solve

Thinking Strategies: Doubles, Doubles Less 1, Doubles Plus 1, and Special Facts

1. Show the problem.

+

2. Think of the answer.

3. Show the sum.

Directions Use math counters to solve each problem. Write the sum in the blank.

5 + 3 = ____ 5 + 5 = ____ 3 + 6 = ____ 4 + 5 = ____ 4 + 4 = ____

5 + 4 = ____ 3 + 3 = ____ 4 + 3 = ____ 6 + 3 = ____ 3 + 5 = ____

Name ______________________ Date ______________

Fast Facts 9

Sums to 10

The activity coordinates with page 27.

5 + 3 = ___ 3 + 4 = ___

3 + 2 = ___ 4 + 5 = ___

4 + 4 = ___ 4 + 3 = ___

3 + 6 = ___ 6 + 3 = ___ 3 + 5 = ___

3 + 3 = ___ 5 + 5 = ___ 5 + 4 = ___

Name ______________________ Date ______________

Fast Facts 10

Sums to 10

The activity coordinates with page 27.

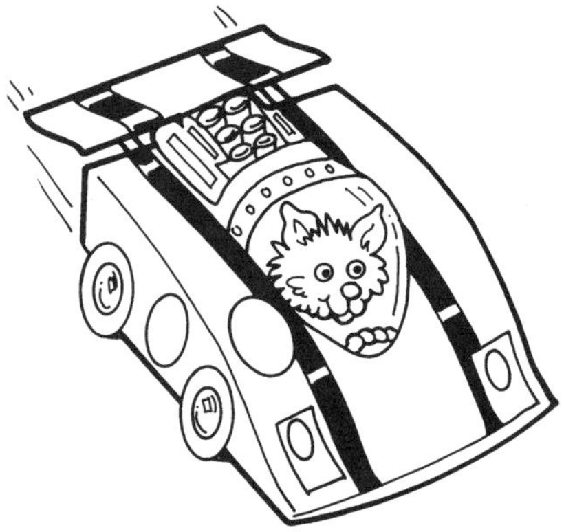

5 + 4 = ___ 4 + 5 = ___

3 + 4 = ___ 3 + 2 = ___

5 + 5 = ___ 5 + 3 = ___

4 + 3 = ___ 3 + 5 = ___ 4 + 4 = ___

3 + 3 = ___ 6 + 3 = ___ 3 + 6 = ___

Name ____________________ Date ____________________

Show and Solve

1 Show the problem.

+

2 Think of the answer.

3 Show the sum.

Directions Use math counters to solve each problem. Write the sum in the blank.

7 + 3 = ___ 5 + 4 = ___ 6 + 4 = ___ 3 + 5 = ___ 4 + 6 = ___

5 + 5 = ___ 5 + 3 = ___ 3 + 7 = ___ 4 + 4 = ___ 4 + 5 = ___

Name ______________________ Date ______________

Fast Facts 11

Sums to 10

The activity coordinates with page 29.

6 + 4 = ___ 3 + 7 = ___

3 + 3 = ___ 4 + 3 = ___

5 + 4 = ___ 7 + 3 = ___

8 + 2 = ___ 5 + 5 = ___ 4 + 6 = ___

4 + 4 = ___ 6 + 3 = ___ 3 + 5 = ___

Name ______________________ Date ______________

Fast Facts 12

Sums to 10

The activity coordinates with page 29.

5 + 5 = ___ 2 + 8 = ___

3 + 6 = ___ 3 + 3 = ___

5 + 3 = ___ 4 + 6 = ___

7 + 3 = ___ 3 + 4 = ___ 4 + 4 = ___

6 + 4 = ___ 4 + 5 = ___ 3 + 7 = ___

Partner Game—Code 10

Getting Ready: Make four copies of this page and one copy of the game board on page 32 on colorful card stock. Cut out the game pieces along the dashed lines. Provide a game marker for each player.

Playing the Game: To begin the game, place the game board in the center of the playing area. Give each player a game marker to set on "Start." Shuffle the game cards, pass out four cards to each player, and then arrange the remaining cards facedown in a pile on the game board. The players turn their cards faceup. Player A begins by looking at the cards and then combines any two numbers to make the sum of 9 or 10.

Rules to Remember:

- If the sum of 9 is made, the game marker is moved one space.
- If the sum of 10 is made, the marker is moved two spaces.
- At the end of the turn, the player discards the two cards that were used and draws two more cards.
- If the sum of 9 or 10 cannot be made, the player may draw one card and then discard one. At that time, if the player still cannot make the designated sum, the player's turn is over.
- Each player is only allowed to have four cards in total.

Player B continues the game in the same manner. When all of the game cards have been used, shuffle the discard pile and turn them facedown in a pile. As a fun twist, the numbers 6 and 9 are interchangeable. The game ends when the first player lands on the words "You Fixed It."

1	2	3	4	5
5	6	7	8	9

Code 10

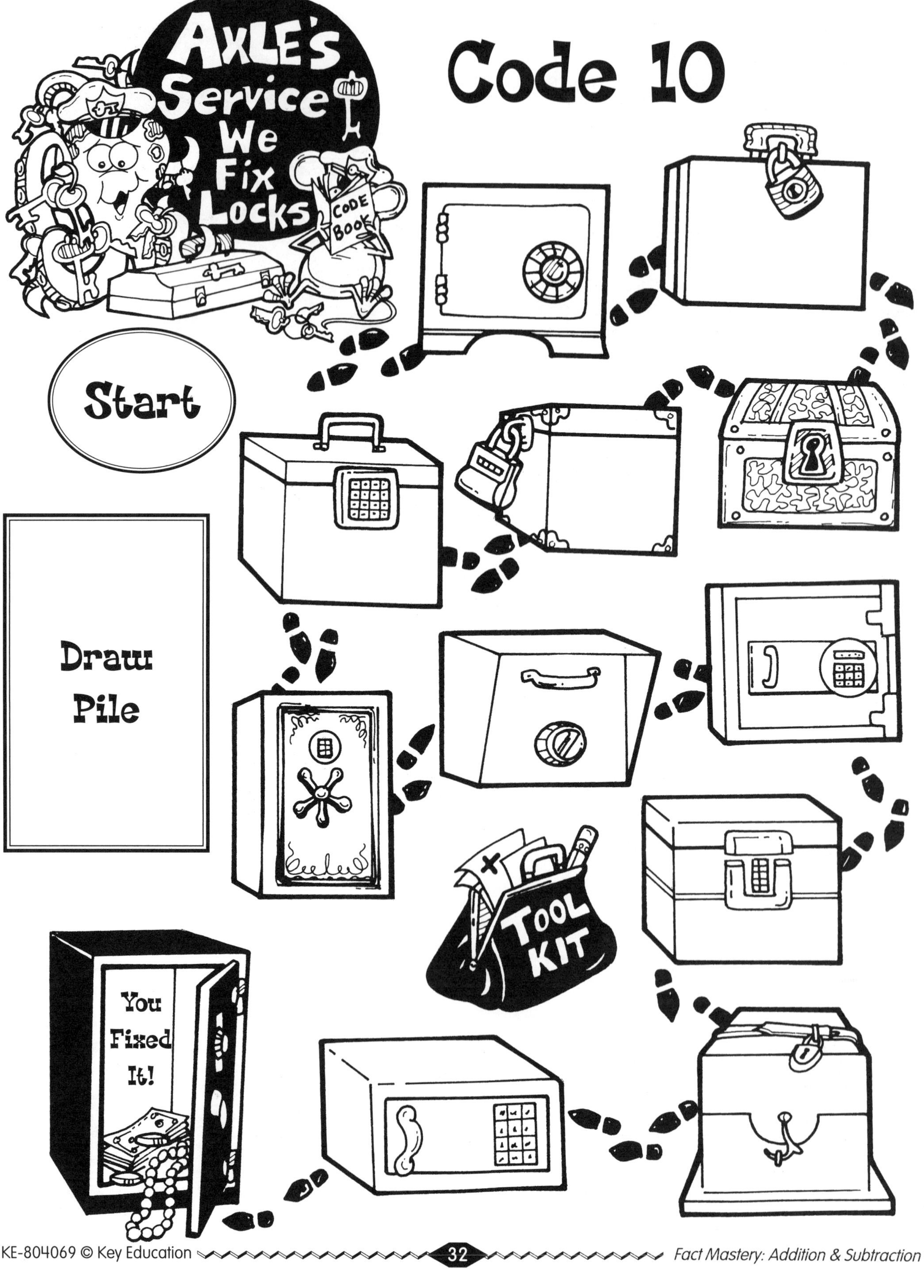
AXLE'S
Service
We
Fix
Locks
CODE BOOK
Start
Draw Pile
TOOL KIT
You Fixed It!

Name ______________________________ Date ____________________

Quick Check E

Sums to 10

The test is on facts from pages 27–30 and previously learned facts. Alternate it with Quick Check F. The new facts are repeated for extra practice.

Score: __________

Time:

A	4 + 6	6 + 3	7 + 3	5 + 4	2 + 4	3 + 5
B	3 + 4	6 + 4	3 + 5	3 + 7	5 + 0	4 + 4
C	3 + 5	7 + 3	1 + 4	3 + 6	6 + 4	2 + 5
D	0 + 5	3 + 3	5 + 5	4 + 5	5 + 3	4 + 6
E	6 + 3	2 + 3	3 + 7	2 + 2	3 + 6	6 + 4
F	5 + 3	1 + 6	4 + 6	2 + 6	1 + 3	2 + 7

Name ______________________ Date ______________

Quick Check F

Sums to 10

The test is on facts from pages 27–30 and previously learned facts. Alternate it with Quick Check E. The new facts are repeated for extra practice.

Score: ______

Time:

A	5 + 2	3 + 7	4 + 3	6 + 4	5 + 3	6 + 3
B	3 + 5	4 + 4	2 + 8	4 + 2	7 + 3	3 + 6
C	6 + 3	4 + 6	5 + 3	5 + 5	3 + 4	6 + 2
D	4 + 3	5 + 4	3 + 7	3 + 5	2 + 3	6 + 4
E	4 + 5	7 + 3	5 + 2	0 + 8	4 + 6	2 + 2
F	3 + 6	3 + 2	4 + 6	2 + 5	7 + 2	5 + 3

Name ____________________ Date ____________________

50 Nifty Facts A

Sums to 10

Alternate this test with page 36.

A	6 + 3	5 + 5	8 + 1	3 + 2	3 + 5
B	1 + 6	2 + 5	6 + 4	4 + 2	7 + 3
C	4 + 3	1 + 7	3 + 3	5 + 4	0 + 9
D	1 + 3	0 + 6	2 + 8	3 + 6	1 + 4
E	4 + 4	1 + 9	5 + 2	4 + 1	0 + 7
F	5 + 1	3 + 4	2 + 6	2 + 4	4 + 5
G	8 + 0	1 + 5	0 + 1	6 + 1	2 + 7
H	2 + 3	4 + 6	0 + 10	2 + 1	8 + 2
I	3 + 1	6 + 2	9 + 1	5 + 3	3 + 7
J	7 + 1	6 + 0	10 + 0	2 + 2	7 + 2

Name ______________________ Date ______________

50 Nifty Facts B

Sums to 10

Alternate this test with page 35.

A	5 + 3	1 + 8	3 + 3	2 + 6	6 + 4
B	0 + 8	7 + 2	4 + 3	8 + 2	1 + 5
C	5 + 5	0 + 7	4 + 1	6 + 3	0 + 5
D	6 + 1	3 + 5	7 + 3	2 + 7	4 + 2
E	6 + 2	1 + 9	0 + 4	5 + 4	2 + 3
F	0 + 10	4 + 4	2 + 4	3 + 1	3 + 6
G	1 + 6	0 + 3	5 + 2	3 + 7	5 + 1
H	3 + 2	7 + 1	4 + 5	2 + 8	3 + 4
I	4 + 6	2 + 5	0 + 9	2 + 2	1 + 7
J	2 + 0	0 + 0	8 + 1	4 + 0	1 + 1

Name ____________________ Date ____________________

Think and Solve

Thinking Strategy:
How Far Apart?
Count Up (+0, +1)

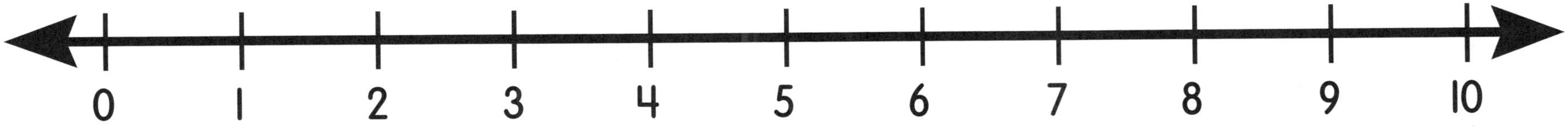

Fold on line.

Directions

- Hide the number line by folding over the top of this paper.
- Work with a partner.
- Read each problem. Then, tell your partner how you will solve it.
- Write the missing addend in the blank.
- Use the number line to check your answers.

9 + ___ = 9	5 + ___ = 6	___ + 4 = 4	2 + ___ = 3	___ + 8 = 8
4 + ___ = 5	___ + 8 = 9	___ + 2 = 2	___ + 3 = 4	7 + ___ = 7
5 + ___ = 5	6 + ___ = 7	9 + ___ = 10	___ + 7 = 8	___ + 6 = 6

Name ______________________ Date ______________

Fast Facts 13

Sums to 10

The activity coordinates with page 37.

___ + 0 = 6   ___ + 4 = 5

9 + ___ = 10   7 + ___ = 8

8 + ___ = 8   ___ + 10 = 10

___ + 2 = 3   ___ + 5 = 6   ___ + 5 = 5

3 + ___ = 4   9 + ___ = 9   6 + ___ = 7

Name ______________________ Date ______________

Fast Facts 14

Sums to 10

The activity coordinates with page 37.

___ + 3 = 3   ___ + 7 = 7

1 + ___ = 2   ___ + 9 = 10

4 + ___ = 5   5 + ___ = 5

8 + ___ = 9   ___ + 3 = 4   ___ + 8 = 9

10 + ___ = 10   4 + ___ = 4   ___ + 1 = 1

Think and Solve

Thinking Strategy:
How Far Apart? Count Up
(+0, +1, +2)

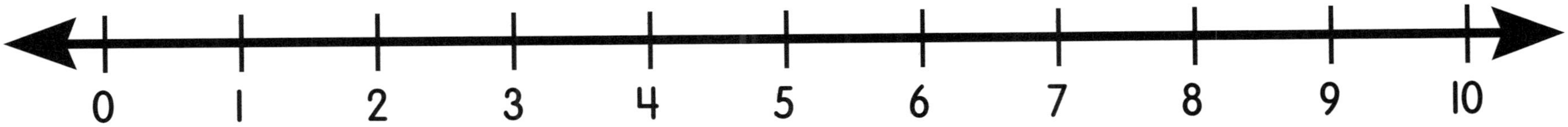

Fold on line.

Directions

- Hide the number line by folding over the top of this paper.
- Work with a partner.
- Read each problem. Then, tell your partner how you will solve it.
- Write the missing addend in the blank.
- Use the number line to check your answers.

2 + ___ = 4	6 + ___ = 7	___ + 5 = 6	___ + 6 = 8	3 + ___ = 5
7 + ___ = 7	___ + 2 = 3	5 + ___ = 7	___ + 8 = 9	2 + ___ = 2
___ + 8 = 10	4 + ___ = 4	___ + 7 = 9	4 + ___ = 6	___ + 3 = 3

Name ______________________ Date ______________

Fast Facts 15

Sums to 10

The activity coordinates with page 39.

___ + 4 = 6   ___ + 5 = 5

8 + ___ = 10   3 + ___ = 5

7 + ___ = 9   7 + ___ = 8

___ + 4 = 4   ___ + 5 = 7   6 + ___ = 8

5 + ___ = 6   ___ + 2 = 4   9 + ___ = 9

Name ______________________ Date ______________

Fast Facts 16

Sums to 10

The activity coordinates with page 39.

___ + 6 = 8   ___ + 6 = 6

4 + ___ = 6   7 + ___ = 9

3 + ___ = 4   4 + ___ = 5

2 + ___ = 4   ___ + 3 = 5   ___ + 8 = 10

___ + 7 = 8   5 + ___ = 7   8 + ___ = 8

Think and Solve

Thinking Strategies:
How Far Apart?
Count Up and Count Back

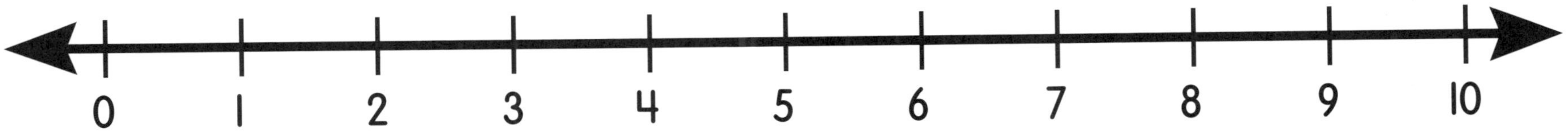

Fold on line.

Directions

- Hide the number line by folding over the top of this paper.
- Work with a partner.
- Read each problem. Then, tell your partner how you will solve it.
- Write the missing addend in the blank.
- Use the number line to check your answers.

3 + ___ = 6	4 + ___ = 7	___ + 8 = 9	4 + ___ = 6	___ + 7 = 9
6 + ___ = 8	___ + 8 = 10	6 + ___ = 9	___ + 5 = 7	7 + ___ = 10
___ + 3 = 8	6 + ___ = 7	___ + 3 = 5	1 + ___ = 4	___ + 2 = 5

Name ____________________ Date ____________________

Fast Facts 17 Sums to 10

The activity coordinates with page 41.

___ + 5 = 7   ___ + 7 = 9

3 + ___ = 6   5 + ___ = 5

___ + 4 = 7   8 + ___ = 9

2 + ___ = 6   ___ + 6 = 9   4 + ___ = 7

7 + ___ = 10   2 + ___ = 10   5 + ___ = 8

Name ____________________ Date ____________________

Fast Facts 18 Sums to 10

The activity coordinates with page 41.

___ + 4 = 5   ___ + 3 = 6

___ + 7 = 10   4 + ___ = 7

3 + ___ = 5   8 + ___ = 9

5 + ___ = 7   7 + ___ = 9   ___ + 5 = 8

6 + ___ = 9   9 + ___ = 10   2 + ___ = 5

Name ______________________ Date ______________

Think and Write

Sums to 10

The activity coordinates with pages 37–42.

9 + ___ = 10   5 + ___ = 8

5 + ___ = 7   ___ + 3 = 6

___ + 4 = 4   8 + ___ = 9   ___ + 7 = 9

4 + ___ = 6   ___ + 6 = 9   ___ + 4 = 5

---

3 + 7 = ___   3 + 2 = ___   8 + 2 = ___

3 + 4 = ___   5 + 2 = ___   6 + 3 = ___

2 + 5 = ___   2 + 6 = ___   2 + 4 = ___

5 + 3 = ___   7 + 2 = ___   3 + 6 = ___

---

3 + ___ = 6   ___ + 2 = 4   6 + ___ = 8

7 + ___ = 10   ___ + 5 = 7   4 + ___ = 7

1 + ___ = 4   2 + ___ = 3   ___ + 8 = 10

___ + 3 = 5   ___ + 5 = 8   ___ + 7 = 8

Think and Solve

Thinking Strategies: Sums of 10, Special Facts, and How Far Apart? Count Up and Count Back

0 1 2 3 4 5 6 7 8 9 10

Fold on line.

Directions

- Hide the number line by folding over the top of this paper.
- Work with a partner.
- Read each problem. Then, tell your partner how you will solve it.
- Write the missing addend in the blank.
- Use the number line to check your answers.

5 + ___ = 10 4 + ___ = 10 7 + ___ = 10 2 + ___ = 10 6 + ___ = 9

9 + ___ = 10 3 + ___ = 10 9 + ___ = 9 ___ + 10 = 10 ___ + 5 = 10

3 + ___ = 9 6 + ___ = 10 8 + ___ = 10 ___ + 0 = 10 1 + ___ = 10

Name ______________________ Date ______________

Fast Facts 19

Sums to 10

The activity coordinates with page 44.

5 + ___ = 10   6 + ___ = 9

___ + 6 = 10   8 + ___ = 10

___ + 3 = 10   ___ + 4 = 10

3 + ___ = 9   3 + ___ = 10   9 + ___ = 10

___ + 9 = 10   2 + ___ = 10   ___ + 0 = 10

Name ______________________ Date ______________

Fast Facts 20

Sums to 10

The activity coordinates with page 44.

2 + ___ = 10   4 + ___ = 10

___ + 6 = 9   ___ + 7 = 10

8 + ___ = 10   1 + ___ = 10

___ + 5 = 10   ___ + 3 = 9   ___ + 10 = 10

9 + ___ = 10   6 + ___ = 10   ___ + 3 = 10

Name ______________________ Date ______________

Think and Solve

Thinking Strategies: Doubles, Special Facts, and How Far Apart? Count Up and Count Back

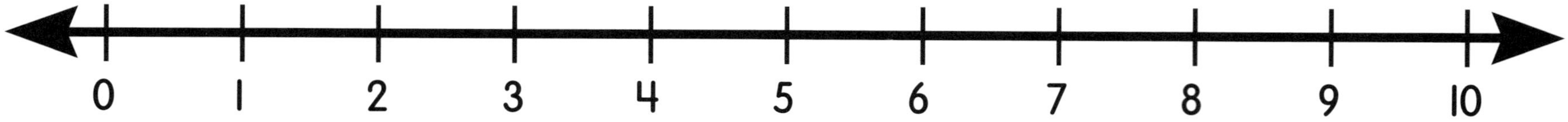

Fold on line.

Directions

- Hide the number line by folding over the top of this paper.
- Work with a partner.
- Read each problem. Then, tell your partner how you will solve it.
- Write the missing addend in the blank.
- Use the number line to check your answers.

3 + ____ = 5	____ + 2 = 4	____ + 2 = 3	3 + ____ = 7	____ + 1 = 3
5 + ____ = 9	4 + ____ = 9	1 + ____ = 2	2 + ____ = 5	4 + ____ = 8
4 + ____ = 7	3 + ____ = 8	____ + 3 = 6	5 + ____ = 8	____ + 5 = 10

Name ________________________ Date ____________

Fast Facts 21 Sums to 10

The activity coordinates with page 46.

4 + ____ = 8 3 + ____ = 7

3 + ____ = 8 ____ + 2 = 4

____ + 5 = 9 5 + ____ = 8

3 + ____ = 6 ____ + 2 = 5 ____ + 3 = 7

____ + 5 = 10 ____ + 4 = 9 2 + ____ = 5

Name ________________________ Date ____________

Fast Facts 22 Sums to 10

The activity coordinates with page 46.

____ + 4 = 7 3 + ____ = 6

3 + ____ = 5 ____ + 4 = 8

4 + ____ = 9 ____ + 2 = 4

____ + 5 = 8 2 + ____ = 3 5 + ____ = 9

5 + ____ = 10 2 + ____ = 5 ____ + 3 = 8

Partner Game—Number Quest

Getting Ready: Make three copies of the number cards below and one copy of the game board on page 49 on colorful card stock. Cut out the game pieces along the dashed lines. Provide 10–12 identical game markers for each player.

Playing the Game: To begin the game, place the game board in the center of the playing area. Sort the number cards into Set A (addends 2–6) and Set B (sums 7–10). Arrange both piles of cards facedown on the game board where indicated. Give each player a set of game markers. To begin the game, Player A turns over the top card in each pile, figures out the missing addend, and then discards the cards. For example, if the math sentence is 2 + ? = 7, the answer is 5. Player A covers the number 5 in one of the boxes. If the answer is already covered, Player A's turn is over. Player B then continues the game in the same manner. As a fun twist, whenever the missing addend is 7 or 8, the player covers two numbers that equal that number. The first player to place game markers on three adjacent boxes in a horizontal, vertical, or diagonal row is the winner.

Make three copies.

Number Quest

\+ ? =

Cover three spaces in a ↑, →, ↗, or ↘ row to win. Note: For missing addend 7 or 8, cover two numbers that equal that number.

2	3	5	6	1	4
4	5	1	3	2	6
5	2	6	4	3	1

Name ______________________ Date ______________

Think and Write

Sums to 10

The activity coordinates with pages 44–47.

2 + ___ = 4 ___ + 3 = 6

4 + ___ = 9 5 + ___ = 10

___ + 3 = 7 ___ + 2 = 5 9 + ___ = 10

6 + ___ = 10 3 + ___ = 8 3 + ___ = 10

---

5 + 3 = ___ 8 + 2 = ___ 4 + 4 = ___

5 + 5 = ___ 3 + 4 = ___ 6 + 4 = ___

3 + 6 = ___ 1 + 2 = ___ 3 + 3 = ___

5 + 4 = ___ 10 + 0 = ___ 7 + 3 = ___

---

2 + ___ = 10 ___ + 3 = 5 4 + ___ = 10

___ + 1 = 2 ___ + 5 = 9 5 + ___ = 8

___ + 4 = 7 7 + ___ = 10 1 + ___ = 10

___ + 10 = 10 2 + ___ = 3 ___ + 3 = 9

Fact Mastery: Minuends to 10

When students have demonstrated mastery of the addition facts with sums to 10, challenge them with activities and timed tests for the related subtraction facts. As each strategy is introduced, print its name in a prominent location. Then, students may refer to the list when solving subtraction problems on the Show and Solve, Think and Solve, and Fast Facts practice pages. *To help students develop the habit of using mental strategies, it is recommended that they verbalize their methods for solving the math problems to their partners.* Point out how it is possible to calculate the answer for a problem in different ways.

Strategies to Introduce and Use

Count Back (–0, –1, –2, –3). When students are subtracting a small number such as 1, 2, or 3, have them count back from the minuend the corresponding subtrahend. To do this, ask the child to make a fist to represent the minuend. Tap the fist with the other hand when saying the minuend *as if you have packed your hand with that number of counters*, and then continue by extending the corresponding fingers while counting back from the minuend. For example, to solve 10 – 3, make a fist, say the number 10 *(tap the fist)*, and then count back 3 *(9, 8, 7—extending a finger for each number)*. Finally, announce the answer as 7.

To help students internalize these number relationships and not depend on counting on their fingers or objects, provide lots of practice on the facts introduced on pages 54, 55, and 59. Pair off students and have them tell each other the answers for subtraction problems that you call out. Alternatively, tell students the rule, such as, "The answer is 2 less." Then, call out numbers randomly from 2 to 10 and have students apply the rule to those numbers. For example, you might say, "What is 2 less than 7?" (The answer would be 5.) Continue in the same manner for other minuends. Encourage students to tell their partners the answers quickly. You might also have students write the featured facts on index cards for additional practice.

How Far Apart? Choose a Strategy. An important question to ask whenever students are reading a subtraction problem is "How far apart are the numbers?" In other words, how far is the subtrahend from the minuend? Are the numbers "close or near neighbors" on a number line? (There would be a difference of 1 or 2 between them.) If the answer to the question is *Yes*, use the mental strategy "Count Up." This is possible by starting at the subtrahend and counting up to the minuend to find the difference. For example, to solve 9 – 7, you would say, "7 *(tap the fist for this number)*, 8 *(extend a finger on the other hand)*, 9 *(extend a second finger)*." The difference would be 2. These facts are introduced on pages 63 and 65.

Think Addition. Provide lots of practice for students to identify the related addition sentences in a fact family. Have students pair off. Call out to the class any of the subtraction problems featured on the Show and Solve, Think and Solve, and Fast Facts pages provided in this section of the book. Have students quickly verbalize the related addition facts with missing addends.

Think Addition and Use Double Facts. When students know the double facts, it is easy for them to apply that knowledge to solve subtraction problems. Demonstrate this strategy by using the related subtraction facts for the double facts. For example, to solve 8 – 4, think 4 + 4 = 8 to find out that the difference would be 4. Continue the exercise by also constructing mental comparisons with the doubles plus 1 and doubles less 1 facts. For example, to solve 9 – 4, think 4 + 4 = 8. By comparing this double fact with 4 + ? = 9, the student now knows that the difference is double plus 1, or 5. Pair off students. Call out math facts from page 71 and have students discuss and solve the problems. You might also have students write the featured facts on index cards for independent study.

Think Addition and Use Sums of 10. If the minuend is 10, think of the related addition fact. Demonstrate this strategy with the problem 10 – 4. To solve it, think of the related addition fact 4 + 6 = 10. You might also have students write these facts on index cards for additional practice. This set of facts includes 10 – 4 and 10 – 6 (on page 71) and 10 – 3 and 10 – 7 (on page 75).

Think Addition and Use Special Facts. For some subtraction facts, there are not clear strategies that can be used to solve them. Sometimes, it is helpful to compare those facts to their related addition facts, doubles, or sums of 10 facts. Direct students to write the subtraction special facts on index cards and practice them frequently. Those facts include 9 – 3, 9 – 6, 8 – 3, 8 – 5, 7 – 4, and 7 – 3 (on page 75).

Name ______________________________ Date ______________

Pretest/Posttest

Score: ________

A	10 − 7	3 − 2	8 − 1	6 − 2	10 − 4	7 − 5	9 − 3
B	8 − 4	10 − 9	6 − 1	9 − 6	7 − 4	9 − 2	4 − 1
C	8 − 2	7 − 0	9 − 5	5 − 4	8 − 8	10 − 3	5 − 1
D	10 − 8	6 − 3	9 − 9	10 − 2	8 − 3	7 − 6	9 − 7
E	7 − 3	10 − 5	5 − 2	7 − 1	6 − 4	8 − 5	9 − 1
F	8 − 6	9 − 0	7 − 2	10 − 6	4 − 2	9 − 4	6 − 5
G	9 − 8	4 − 4	5 − 3	6 − 0	10 − 1	8 − 7	4 − 3

Progress Chart

Minuends to 10

Name	Quick Check A	Quick Check B	Quick Check C	Quick Check D	Quick Check E	Quick Check F	Quick Check G	Quick Check H	50 Facts A	50 Facts B

Show and Solve

Thinking Strategy:
Count Back (−0, −1)

1. Show the problem.

2. Think of the difference for the problem and write it down. Take away the correct number of math counters and put them on the drawing to check your answer.

Directions

- Read each problem and solve it.
- If needed, use math counters and follow the steps above.

1 − 0 = ___	8 − 0 = ___	2 − 1 = ___	6 − 1 = ___	9 − 0 = ___
7 − 1 = ___	3 − 1 = ___	6 − 0 = ___	2 − 0 = ___	4 − 1 = ___
5 − 1 = ___	7 − 0 = ___	8 − 1 = ___	5 − 0 = ___	9 − 1 = ___

Show and Solve

Thinking Strategy:
Count Back (−1, −2)

1 Show the problem.

2 Think of the difference for the problem and write it down. Take away the correct number of math counters and put them on the drawing to check your answer.

Directions

- Read each problem and solve it.
- If needed, use math counters and follow the steps above.

$6 - 2 =$ ___	$1 - 1 =$ ___	$5 - 2 =$ ___	$9 - 1 =$ ___	$3 - 2 =$ ___
$8 - 1 =$ ___	$7 - 2 =$ ___	$6 - 1 =$ ___	$8 - 2 =$ ___	$10 - 2 =$ ___
$2 - 2 =$ ___	$10 - 1 =$ ___	$9 - 2 =$ ___	$5 - 1 =$ ___	$7 - 1 =$ ___

Name ______________________ Date ______________

Fast Facts 23

Minuends to 10

The activity coordinates with pages 54 and 55.

10 − 1 = ___ 5 − 1 = ___

7 − 0 = ___ 4 − 2 = ___

4 − 1 = ___ 8 − 1 = ___

6 − 2 = ___ 9 − 0 = ___ 1 − 1 = ___

8 − 2 = ___ 7 − 2 = ___ 6 − 0 = ___

Name ______________________ Date ______________

Fast Facts 24

Minuends to 10

The activity coordinates with pages 54 and 55.

3 − 2 = ___ 3 − 1 = ___

5 − 2 = ___ 10 − 2 = ___

9 − 1 = ___ 6 − 1 = ___

5 − 0 = ___ 8 − 0 = ___ 10 − 0 = ___

2 − 1 = ___ 9 − 2 = ___ 7 − 1 = ___

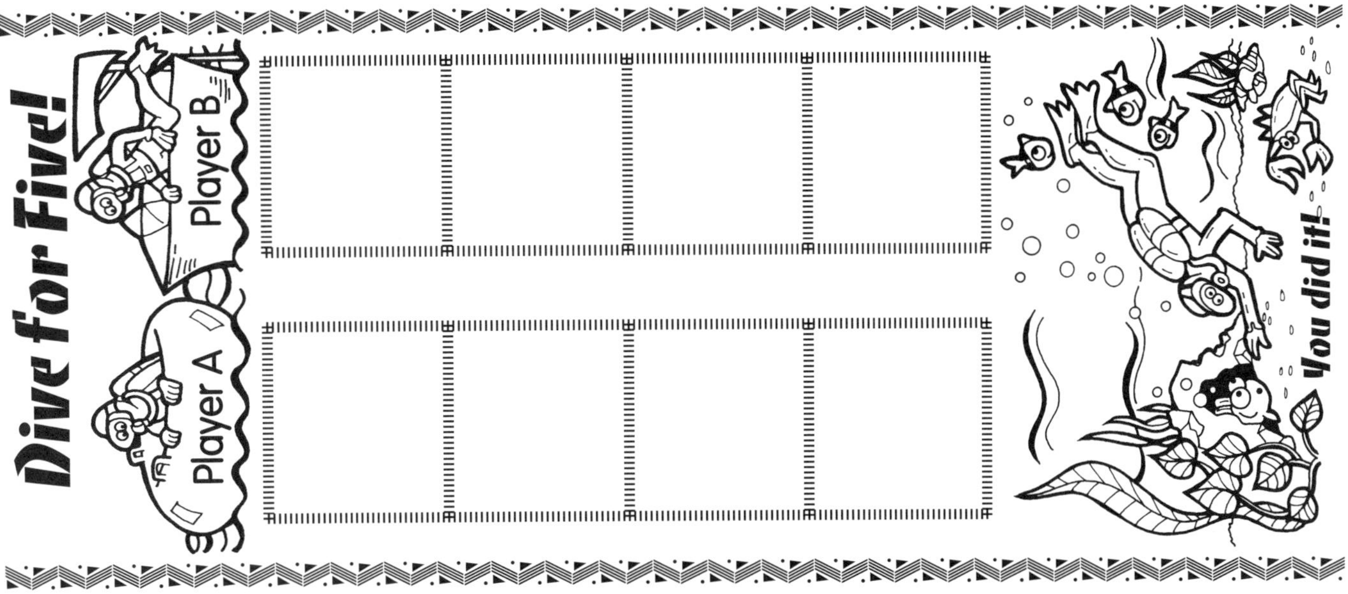

Partner Game—Dive for Five!

Getting Ready: Copy this page and the numeral cards on page 58 onto colorful card stock. Cut out the game pieces along the dashed lines. To form the die, fold along the solid lines to make the cube shape and then glue the tabs as indicated under the numerals. Tape the edges of the cube for durability. Provide two game markers.

Playing the Game: Scatter the numeral cards facedown in the center of the playing area. Player A places a game marker on the inner tube or boat, rolls the die, and then draws one game card. When the card is turned faceup, the player must subtract the number shown on the die from the game card and *say the subtraction sentence out loud.* Player B should listen carefully for errors. If the answer is correct, Player A moves the game marker down to the first box on the game board. If the answer is incorrect, Player A may not move the game marker. Player B takes a turn and continues the game in the same manner. If the words "Go back to the boat!" are rolled, the player must move the game marker back to the boat or inner tube. All of the numeral cards are returned facedown to the playing area whenever they are needed. The game ends when one or both players reach the bottom of the sea.

Subtrahend Die

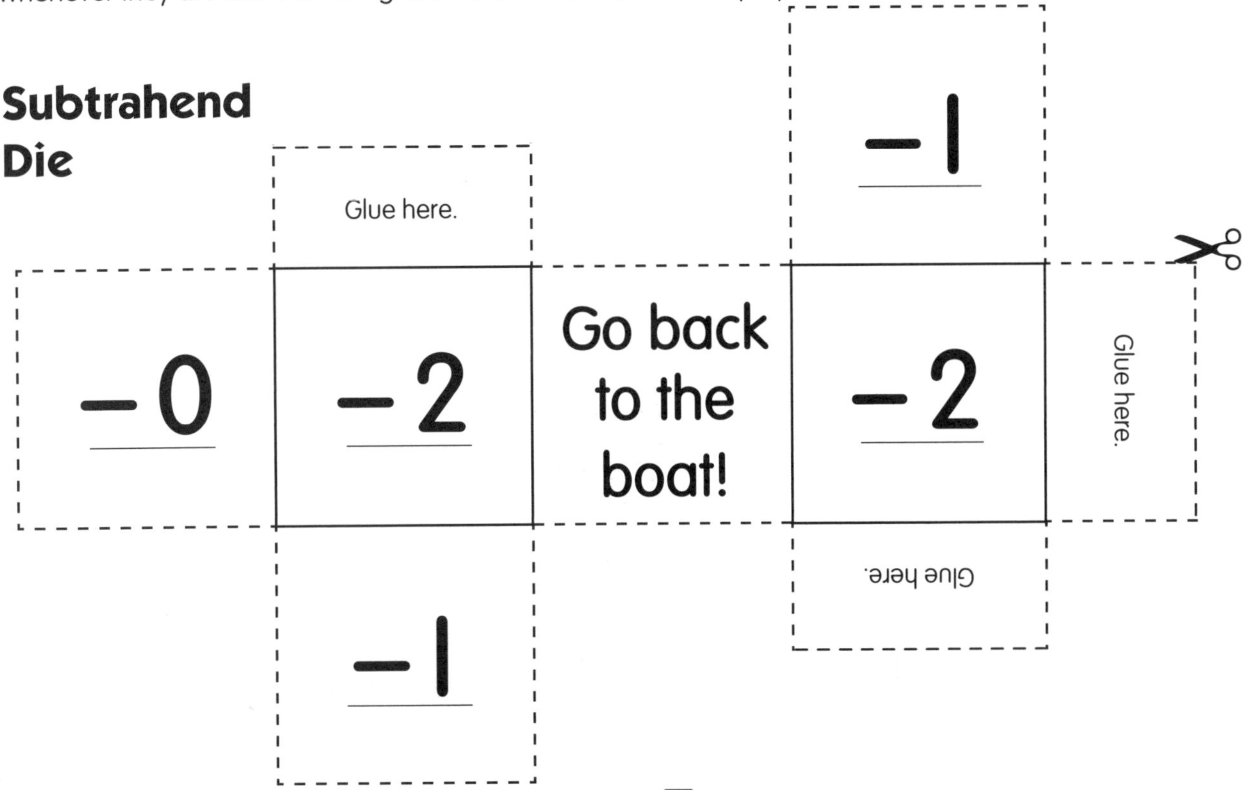

2

3

4

5

6

7

8

9

10

10

Think and Solve

Thinking Strategy:
Count Back (−2, −3)

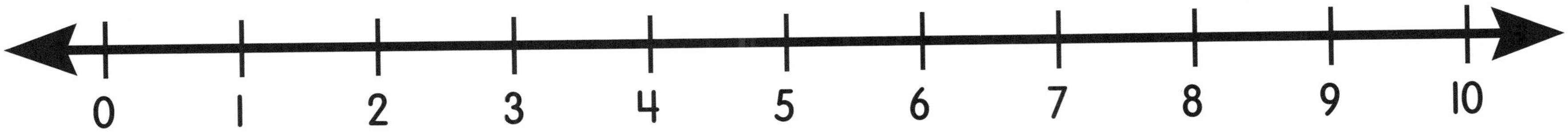

Fold on line.

Directions

- Hide the number line by folding over the top of this paper.
- Work with a partner.
- Read each problem. Then, tell your partner how you will solve it.
- Write the difference (answer) in the blank.
- Use the number line to check your answers.

3 − 3 = ___	9 − 2 = ___	8 − 3 = ___	5 − 2 = ___	10 − 3 = ___
7 − 2 = ___	6 − 3 = ___	10 − 2 = ___	7 − 3 = ___	4 − 3 = ___
9 − 3 = ___	5 − 3 = ___	3 − 2 = ___	8 − 2 = ___	6 − 2 = ___

Name ______________________________ Date ______________

Fast Facts 25

Minuends to 10

The activity coordinates with page 59.

9 – 3 = ___ 8 – 2 = ___

2 – 2 = ___ 5 – 3 = ___

6 – 2 = ___ 8 – 3 = ___

3 – 3 = ___ 10 – 2 = ___ 4 – 3 = ___

3 – 2 = ___ 7 – 3 = ___ 10 – 3 = ___

Name ______________________________ Date ______________

Fast Facts 26

Minuends to 10

The activity coordinates with page 59.

3 – 3 = ___ 7 – 3 = ___

6 – 3 = ___ 4 – 3 = ___

8 – 3 = ___ 9 – 3 = ___

5 – 3 = ___ 4 – 2 = ___ 5 – 2 = ___

7 – 2 = ___ 10 – 3 = ___ 9 – 2 = ___

Name ______________________ Date ______________

Quick Check A

Minuends to 10

The test is on facts from pages 54–60. Alternate it with Quick Check B.

Score: ____________

Time:

A	1 − 0	10 − 1	4 − 2	8 − 3	5 − 0	6 − 3
B	7 − 2	4 − 1	9 − 3	2 − 0	1 − 1	5 − 2
C	8 − 1	3 − 1	10 − 2	7 − 3	8 − 0	2 − 1
D	10 − 3	9 − 0	6 − 1	3 − 2	5 − 3	9 − 1
E	4 − 3	7 − 1	2 − 2	6 − 0	9 − 2	5 − 1
F	7 − 0	4 − 0	8 − 2	3 − 3	10 − 0	6 − 2

Name ______________________________ Date ________________

Quick Check B

Minuends to 10

The test is on facts from pages 54–60. Alternate it with Quick Check A.

Score: ____________

Time:

A	0 − 0	9 − 3	6 − 2	1 − 1	10 − 2	4 − 3
B	4 − 1	8 − 0	3 − 3	2 − 2	6 − 1	8 − 2
C	10 − 3	2 − 1	9 − 2	7 − 1	2 − 0	8 − 3
D	5 − 2	3 − 0	10 − 0	7 − 2	5 − 3	10 − 1
E	8 − 1	7 − 3	3 − 1	5 − 0	4 − 2	5 − 1
F	3 − 2	6 − 3	7 − 0	9 − 1	1 − 0	4 − 0

Name ____________ Date ____________

Think and Solve

Thinking Strategies:
How Far Apart?
Count Up and Count Back

Fold on line.

Directions

- Hide the number line by folding over the top of this paper.
- Work with a partner.
- Read each problem. Then, tell your partner how you will solve it.
- Write the difference (answer) in the blank.
- Use the number line to check your answers.

9 – 8 = ___	6 – 6 = ___	4 – 3 = ___	8 – 0 = ___	3 – 2 = ___
4 – 0 = ___	8 – 8 = ___	6 – 5 = ___	10 – 9 = ___	7 – 6 = ___
8 – 1 = ___	5 – 4 = ___	9 – 9 = ___	8 – 7 = ___	0 – 0 = ___

Name ______________________ Date ______________

Fast Facts 27

Minuends to 10

The activity coordinates with page 63.

7 − 7 = ___ 4 − 4 = ___

6 − 1 = ___ 7 − 6 = ___

5 − 4 = ___ 5 − 0 = ___

8 − 1 = ___ 2 − 1 = ___ 8 − 8 = ___

10 − 0 = ___ 8 − 7 = ___ 3 − 2 = ___

Name ______________________ Date ______________

Fast Facts 28

Minuends to 10

The activity coordinates with page 63.

10 − 9 = ___ 9 − 0 = ___

2 − 2 = ___ 6 − 5 = ___

9 − 8 = ___ 4 − 3 = ___

7 − 1 = ___ 3 − 0 = ___ 9 − 9 = ___

5 − 5 = ___ 7 − 6 = ___ 6 − 6 = ___

Name ____________________ Date ____________

Think and Solve

Thinking Strategies:
How Far Apart?
Count Up and Count Back

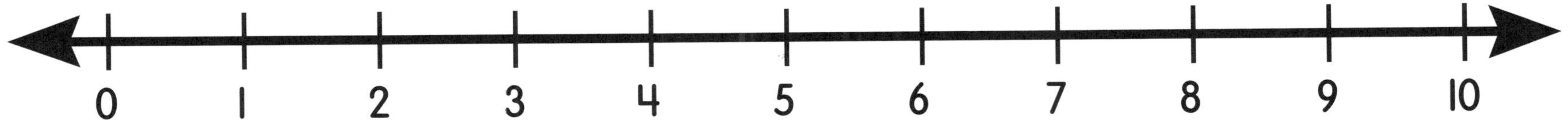

Fold on line.

Directions

- Hide the number line by folding over the top of this paper.
- Work with a partner.
- Read each problem. Then, tell your partner how you will solve it.
- Write the difference (answer) in the blank.
- Use the number line to check your answers.

5 − 3 = ___	9 − 1 = ___	10 − 9 = ___	4 − 2 = ___	7 − 5 = ___
6 − 4 = ___	7 − 2 = ___	9 − 7 = ___	3 − 2 = ___	9 − 8 = ___
9 − 2 = ___	10 − 8 = ___	6 − 2 = ___	3 − 1 = ___	8 − 6 = ___

Name ____________________ Date ____________

Fast Facts 29

Minuends to 10

The activity coordinates with page 65.

$6 - 2 =$ ___ $7 - 5 =$ ___

$9 - 7 =$ ___ $10 - 2 =$ ___

$6 - 4 =$ ___ $5 - 3 =$ ___

$8 - 7 =$ ___ $10 - 8 =$ ___ $3 - 2 =$ ___

$8 - 2 =$ ___ $6 - 5 =$ ___ $8 - 6 =$ ___

Name ____________________ Date ____________

Fast Facts 30

Minuends to 10

The activity coordinates with page 65.

$9 - 8 =$ ___ $5 - 3 =$ ___

$6 - 4 =$ ___ $9 - 2 =$ ___

$4 - 1 =$ ___ $4 - 3 =$ ___

$5 - 2 =$ ___ $8 - 6 =$ ___ $7 - 5 =$ ___

$10 - 8 =$ ___ $7 - 2 =$ ___ $9 - 7 =$ ___

Partner Game—Splash!

Getting Ready: Copy the subtraction game cards below and the game board on page 68 onto colorful card stock. Cut out the game pieces along the dashed lines. Provide three to five identical game markers for each player. Before starting the game, determine how many markers each player will move into the pool.

Playing the Game: To begin the game, place the game board in the center of the playing area. Give each player several game markers to set on the "towels." Shuffle the game cards and place them facedown in a pile near the game board. Player A draws a card and answers the fact. The player places a game marker on "Start" and moves it the same number of spaces on the path as the difference. For example, if the problem is 9 – 7 = 2, the player moves the game marker 2 spaces. Player B then continues the game in the same manner. If the card "Go to the nearest slide. Splash!" is drawn, the player may move a game marker that is either on the path or on the towel into the pool. The first player to move all of the game markers into the pool is declared the winner.

9 – 8	8 – 6	7 – 3	5 – 4	4 – 2	Go to the nearest slide. Splash!
7 – 2	8 – 7	7 – 5	6 – 3	Go to the nearest slide. Splash!	Go to the nearest slide. Splash!
10 – 8	6 – 2	7 – 6	6 – 4	5 – 2	3 – 0
10 – 9	9 – 7	8 – 5	6 – 5	5 – 3	4 – 1

Splash!
Player A: Start here.
Player B: Start here.
Player A
Player B

Name ______________________________ Date ____________________

Quick Check C

Minuends to 10

The test is on facts from pages 63–66 and previously learned facts. Alternate it with Quick Check D.

Score: ____________

Time:

A	$4 - 2$	$6 - 0$	$5 - 4$	$7 - 1$	$10 - 8$	$9 - 9$
B	$5 - 1$	$7 - 5$	$8 - 8$	$9 - 2$	$2 - 0$	$4 - 3$
C	$8 - 2$	$7 - 0$	$3 - 1$	$10 - 9$	$6 - 6$	$5 - 3$
D	$4 - 4$	$9 - 7$	$3 - 2$	$7 - 6$	$6 - 2$	$10 - 0$
E	$5 - 5$	$4 - 0$	$7 - 2$	$8 - 6$	$6 - 5$	$9 - 8$
F	$8 - 7$	$5 - 2$	$4 - 1$	$7 - 7$	$6 - 4$	$3 - 3$

Name ______________________ Date ______________

Quick Check D

Minuends to 10

The test is on facts from pages 63–66 and previously learned facts. Alternate it with Quick Check C.

Score: ______

Time:

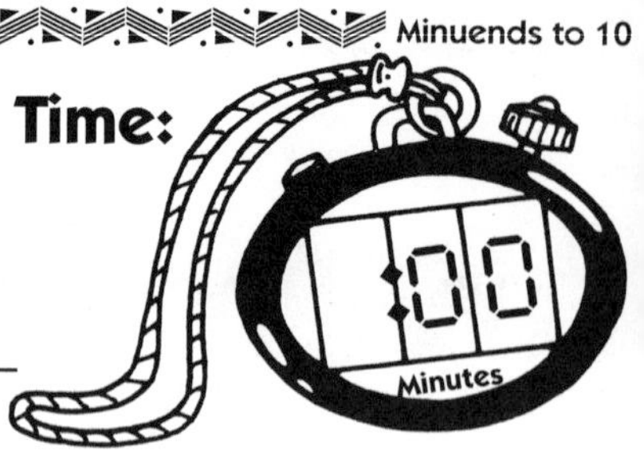

A	5 − 3	10 − 9	7 − 0	10 − 2	6 − 6	9 − 8
B	4 − 4	9 − 7	4 − 0	6 − 4	10 − 10	7 − 2
C	9 − 2	4 − 3	7 − 7	8 − 0	6 − 5	8 − 6
D	8 − 7	9 − 1	4 − 2	7 − 6	8 − 8	3 − 2
E	9 − 9	7 − 5	6 − 0	8 − 1	2 − 1	5 − 2
F	10 − 8	6 − 2	5 − 5	8 − 2	5 − 4	9 − 0

Name ________________ Date ________________

Think and Solve

Thinking Strategies: Think Addition and Use Double Facts and Sums of 10

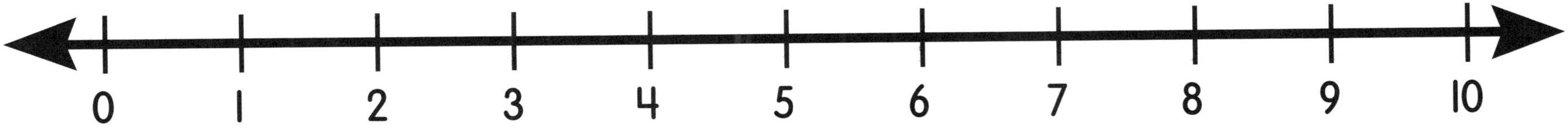

Fold on line.

Directions

- Hide the number line by folding over the top of this paper.
- Work with a partner.
- Read each problem. Then, tell your partner how you will solve it.
- Write the difference (answer) in the blank.
- Use the number line to check your answers.

8 − 4 = ____ 10 − 5 = ____ 10 − 4 = ____

10 − 6 = ____ 6 − 3 = ____ 6 − 2 = ____ 6 − 4 = ____ 10 − 2 = ____

10 − 3 = ____ 10 − 7 = ____ 4 − 2 = ____ 10 − 8 = ____

Name ______________________ Date ____________

Fast Facts 31 Minuends to 10

The activity coordinates with page 71.

10 – 5 = ___ 10 – 6 = ___

6 – 3 = ___ 8 – 4 = ___

10 – 2 = ___ 6 – 2 = ___

10 – 4 = ___ 10 – 8 = ___ 10 – 3 = ___

4 – 2 = ___ 6 – 4 = ___ 10 – 7 = ___

Name ______________________ Date ____________

Fast Facts 32 Minuends to 10

The activity coordinates with page 71.

6 – 4 = ___ 10 – 5 = ___

10 – 3 = ___ 10 – 8 = ___

6 – 3 = ___ 4 – 2 = ___

8 – 4 = ___ 10 – 4 = ___ 10 – 7 = ___

10 – 6 = ___ 6 – 2 = ___ 10 – 2 = ___

Name ______________________ Date ______________

Quick Check E

Minuends to 10

The test is on facts from page 71 and previously learned facts. Alternate it with Quick Check F. The new facts are repeated for extra practice.

Score: __________

Time:

A	10 − 5	10 − 4	8 − 4	10 − 7	6 − 3	6 − 4
B	5 − 4	1 − 1	10 − 8	8 − 6	5 − 5	10 − 3
C	7 − 6	6 − 2	10 − 5	10 − 6	9 − 2	8 − 7
D	7 − 1	10 − 4	9 − 7	8 − 4	4 − 2	6 − 5
E	3 − 1	10 − 3	5 − 2	10 − 9	7 − 5	6 − 3
F	10 − 6	5 − 3	8 − 0	10 − 2	6 − 1	10 − 7

Name ____________________ Date ____________

Quick Check F

Minuends to 10

The test is on facts from page 71 and previously learned facts. Alternate it with Quick Check E. The new facts are repeated for extra practice.

Score: ________

Time:

A	8 − 4	9 − 9	10 − 5	6 − 0	8 − 1	10 − 4
B	10 − 8	10 − 3	10 − 6	8 − 6	10 − 5	10 − 10
C	10 − 1	9 − 2	10 − 7	5 − 4	4 − 4	9 − 8
D	5 − 2	10 − 4	8 − 8	5 − 0	10 − 6	7 − 2
E	10 − 7	3 − 3	4 − 1	10 − 2	7 − 5	8 − 2
F	8 − 4	6 − 2	7 − 6	5 − 1	7 − 0	10 − 3

Think and Solve

Thinking Strategies: Think Addition and Use Double Facts, Sums of 10, and Special Facts

Fold on line.

Directions

- Hide the number line by folding over the top of this paper.
- Work with a partner.
- Read each problem. Then, tell your partner how you will solve it.
- Write the answer in the blank.
- Use the number line to check your answers.

6 + 3 = ___	9 − 3 = ___	3 + 6 = ___	9 − 6 = ___	10 − 5 = ___
8 − 4 = ___	5 + 3 = ___	8 − 3 = ___	3 + 5 = ___	8 − 5 = ___
4 + 5 = ___	9 − 5 = ___	5 + 4 = ___	9 − 4 = ___	
4 + 3 = ___	7 − 3 = ___	3 + 4 = ___	7 − 4 = ___	

Name ______________________ Date ______________

Fast Facts 33

Minuends to 10

The activity coordinates with page 75.

9 – 3 = ___

9 – 4 = ___

6 – 3 = ___

9 – 6 = ___

8 – 3 = ___

10 – 4 = ___

9 – 5 = ___

10 – 5 = ___

7 – 3 = ___

7 – 4 = ___

8 – 4 = ___

8 – 5 = ___

Name ______________________ Date ______________

Fast Facts 34

Minuends to 10

The activity coordinates with page 75.

9 – 3 = ___

8 – 3 = ___

10 – 5 = ___

9 – 4 = ___

9 – 6 = ___

8 – 5 = ___

8 – 4 = ___

7 – 4 = ___

6 – 3 = ___

7 – 3 = ___

9 – 5 = ___

10 – 6 = ___

Name ____________________ Date ____________

Fast Facts 35

Minuends to 10

The activity provides more practice on new facts and coordinates with pages 71 and 75.

10 – 3 = ___ 9 – 5 = ___

10 – 5 = ___ 10 – 7 = ___

9 – 3 = ___ 8 – 5 = ___

10 – 6 = ___ 9 – 6 = ___ 10 – 4 = ___

8 – 4 = ___ 8 – 3 = ___ 9 – 4 = ___

Name ____________________ Date ____________

Fast Facts 36

Minuends to 10

The activity provides more practice on new facts and coordinates with pages 71 and 75.

10 – 4 = ___ 7 – 4 = ___

9 – 6 = ___ 9 – 3 = ___

8 – 5 = ___ 10 – 5 = ___

10 – 7 = ___ 9 – 4 = ___ 10 – 6 = ___

8 – 3 = ___ 10 – 3 = ___ 9 – 5 = ___

Partner Game—Flip 'n' Solve

Getting Ready: Make three copies of the game cards below and one copy of the game board on page 79 on colorful card stock. Cut out the game pieces along the dashed lines. Provide 10 identical game markers for each player.

Playing the Game: To begin the game, place the game board in the center of the playing area. Give each player a set of game markers. Shuffle the game cards and place them facedown in a pile near the game board. Player A draws two cards and places them on the game board to make a subtraction sentence. Player A must verbalize the math sentence and then cover the correct answer on the game board. Player B should listen carefully to catch any errors. If the answer is incorrect or if it is already covered, Player A's turn is over. Player B then continues the game in the same manner. If the card "Cover any space!" is drawn, the player places a game marker accordingly. As a fun twist, the numbers 6 and 9 are interchangeable. The first player to cover all 10 spaces in the row is declared the winner.

Make three copies.

Flip 'n' Solve

Player A

0	1	2	3	4	5	6	7	8	9

Player B

0	1	2	3	4	5	6	7	8	9

Name ______________________ Date ______________

Quick Check G

Minuends to 10

The test is on facts from pages 75–77 and previously learned facts. Alternate it with Quick Check H. The new facts are repeated for extra practice.

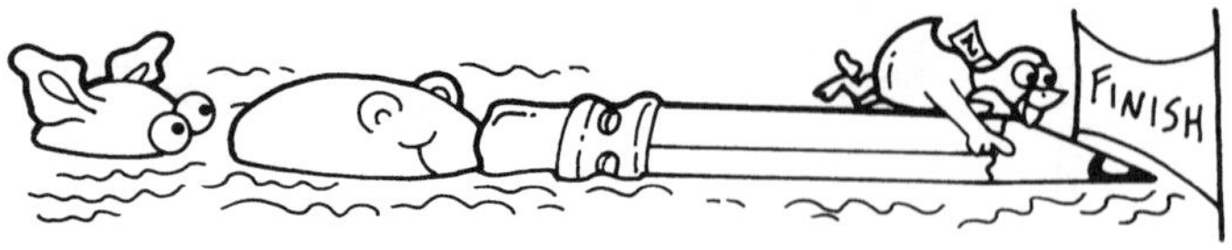

Score: ________

Time:

A	9 − 4	4 − 2	8 − 4	9 − 6	10 − 5	6 − 6
B	7 − 4	9 − 3	6 − 5	3 − 3	10 − 7	8 − 5
C	10 − 6	9 − 1	8 − 3	7 − 2	9 − 5	7 − 3
D	9 − 3	10 − 4	7 − 3	9 − 7	7 − 5	9 − 6
E	8 − 3	3 − 0	8 − 5	3 − 2	9 − 5	10 − 8
F	7 − 4	9 − 4	2 − 1	8 − 0	8 − 3	7 − 7

Name ______________________ Date ______________

Quick Check H

Minuends to 10

The test is on facts from pages 75–77 and previously learned facts. Alternate it with Quick Check G. The new facts are repeated for extra practice.

Score: ____________

Time:

A	7 − 3	9 − 6	8 − 2	5 − 0	10 − 7	6 − 2
B	10 − 3	5 − 1	6 − 3	9 − 8	7 − 4	9 − 3
C	4 − 0	10 − 8	9 − 6	5 − 2	9 − 3	6 − 1
D	9 − 4	10 − 9	8 − 5	7 − 3	6 − 4	8 − 3
E	7 − 4	7 − 1	9 − 5	10 − 2	5 − 4	8 − 8
F	8 − 5	7 − 7	9 − 4	8 − 3	9 − 5	9 − 0

Name ______________________ Date ______________

50 Nifty Facts A

Minuends to 10

Alternate this test with page 83.

A	10 − 5	8 − 6	7 − 3	10 − 10	9 − 6
B	9 − 7	8 − 4	6 − 2	10 − 8	9 − 2
C	5 − 3	10 − 7	9 − 5	10 − 6	7 − 5
D	3 − 2	9 − 1	5 − 0	4 − 2	7 − 7
E	6 − 4	8 − 5	10 − 3	7 − 2	9 − 4
F	10 − 2	7 − 6	8 − 0	4 − 1	5 − 2
G	8 − 1	10 − 4	6 − 5	8 − 3	6 − 1
H	10 − 9	3 − 1	8 − 7	9 − 8	6 − 6
I	9 − 3	7 − 1	7 − 4	8 − 2	4 − 3
J	5 − 4	6 − 3	10 − 1	5 − 1	5 − 5

Name ______________________ Date ______________

50 Nifty Facts B

Minuends to 10

Alternate this test with page 82.

A	8 − 5	3 − 3	9 − 3	10 − 9	7 − 4
B	6 − 5	10 − 5	7 − 1	6 − 3	8 − 2
C	10 − 0	8 − 3	10 − 2	5 − 5	10 − 4
D	7 − 3	6 − 6	7 − 6	9 − 6	5 − 2
E	3 − 2	5 − 3	6 − 4	9 − 8	10 − 3
F	6 − 2	8 − 1	9 − 5	4 − 3	7 − 7
G	10 − 6	8 − 8	8 − 4	4 − 4	10 − 8
H	8 − 6	9 − 2	10 − 10	7 − 5	9 − 4
I	5 − 4	7 − 0	4 − 2	10 − 1	9 − 0
J	6 − 1	9 − 7	4 − 0	7 − 2	9 − 9

Fact Mastery: Sums 11 to 20

Several of the strategies used to solve the facts with sums to 10 can also be used to learn the facts with sums 11 to 20. As each strategy is introduced, print its name in a prominent location. Then, students may refer to the list when solving addition problems on the Show and Solve, Think and Solve, and Fast Facts practice pages. *To help students develop the habit of using mental strategies, it is recommended that they verbalize their methods for solving the math problems to their partners.* Point out how it is possible to calculate the answer for a problem in different ways.

Strategies to Introduce and Use

Switch the Order of Addends. Not all problems will list the larger addend first. Help students learn to recognize when it is necessary to switch the order of the addends mentally to solve the problems. Pair off students. Call out math facts and have students tell each other the larger addend and restate the math problem, if necessary, so that the larger number is mentioned first. Use the facts introduced on pages 87, 89, 93, 106, and 110.

Make 10 and Add What's Left. To apply this strategy, mentally partition the second addend by taking from it the number that when added to the first addend makes 10. Then, add what is left of the second addend to the 10 to arrive at the answer. For example, to solve 9 + 3, take 1 from the addend 3 and add it to 9 to make a sum of 10 (9 + 1 = 10). Finally, add the remaining 2 to the 10 to produce the answer of 12. Have students pair off and solve the problems you call out. Use the facts introduced on pages 87, 89, 93, 106, and 110.

Doubles, Doubles. When students know the double facts, it is easy for them to apply that knowledge to solve other basic addition problems. Have students write the double facts on index cards for additional practice. Use the facts introduced on page 99.

Doubles Less 1. For this strategy, direct students to double the first addend of the given problem to make the double fact and then compare the problems. For example, if 6 + 6 = 12, then the sum for 6 + 5 will be 1 less than 12, which is 11. Have students pair off and solve the problems that you call out. Use the facts introduced on page 99. You might also have students write those facts on index cards for additional practice.

Doubles Plus 1. For this strategy, direct students to make the double fact and then compare the addends. For example, if 6 + 6 = 12, then the sum for 6 + 7 will be 1 more than 12, which is 13. Have students pair off and solve the problems that you call out. Use the facts introduced on page 99. Students may write those facts on index cards for additional drill.

How Far Apart? Choose a Strategy. When working with missing addends, students need to think about how far the given addend is from the sum before choosing a strategy to solve the problem. Are those numbers "next door neighbors"? If *yes,* students can apply the "Count Up" strategy to calculate the answer. If not, they could use the "Count Back" strategy. For example, to solve _ + 2 = 11, count back 2 numbers from 11 to determine that the missing addend is 9. Another mental strategy would be to double the given addend and then compare numbers. For example, to solve 8 + _ = 17, think 8 + 8 = 16 and then calculate that the missing addend needs to be 1 more than 8, which is 9, to make the sum of 17. Have students pair off for the mental math activities. Call out various missing addend problems for them to discuss and solve. Use the problems listed on pages 118, 120, and 125.

Make 10—How Much More Is Needed? Here is another strategy that can be used when working with missing addends. Students can also think of sums of 10 and then calculate how much more is needed so that the addends equal the sum of the problem. For example, to solve _ + 9 = 12, determine that 9 + 1 = 10 and that 2 more are needed to make the sum of 12. The missing addend is 3 (3 + 9 = 12). Have students pair off for the mental math activities. Call out various missing addend problems for them to discuss and solve. Use the problems listed on pages 120, 123, and 125.

Name ____________________ Date ____________

Sums 11 to 20

Pretest/Posttest

Score: ________

A	11 + 0	9 + 9	7 + 4	1 + 10	4 + 8	6 + 5	9 + 6
B	10 + 9	8 + 7	9 + 5	3 + 8	7 + 6	2 + 9	10 + 3
C	8 + 5	7 + 10	6 + 6	4 + 9	5 + 7	6 + 9	9 + 8
D	10 + 8	6 + 7	7 + 9	5 + 8	14 + 0	8 + 4	9 + 3
E	3 + 9	8 + 6	7 + 5	9 + 2	8 + 8	5 + 6	8 + 9
F	5 + 9	6 + 10	8 + 3	9 + 7	10 + 4	7 + 7	5 + 10
G	4 + 7	10 + 10	6 + 8	9 + 10	7 + 8	10 + 2	9 + 4

Progress Chart

Sums 11 to 20

Name	Quick Check A	Quick Check B	Quick Check C	Quick Check D	Quick Check E	Quick Check F	Quick Check G	Quick Check H	Quick Check I	Quick Check J	50 Facts A	50 Facts B

Name ____________ Date ____________

Show and Solve

Thinking Strategies: Switch the Order and Make 10 and Add What's Left

1 Show the problem.

+

2 Think of the answer.

3 Show the sum.

Directions Use math counters to solve each problem. Circle the larger number. Write the sum in the blank.

10 + 1 = ___	1 + 9 = ___	2 + 10 = ___	9 + 2 = ___
3 + 10 = ___	9 + 3 = ___	1 + 10 = ___	9 + 1 = ___
2 + 9 = ___	10 + 2 = ___	10 + 3 = ___	3 + 9 = ___

Name ______________________ Date ______________

Fast Facts 37

Sums 11 to 20

The activity coordinates with page 87.

3 + 9 = ___ 9 + 3 = ___

2 + 10 = ___ 10 + 3 = ___

2 + 9 = ___ 9 + 1 = ___

10 + 1 = ___ 10 + 2 = ___ 3 + 10 = ___

1 + 9 = ___ 1 + 10 = ___ 9 + 2 = ___

Name ______________________ Date ______________

Fast Facts 38

Sums 11 to 20

The activity coordinates with page 87.

2 + 9 = ___ 3 + 9 = ___

9 + 1 = ___ 9 + 2 = ___

2 + 10 = ___ 10 + 1 = ___

1 + 10 = ___ 10 + 2 = ___ 9 + 3 = ___

10 + 3 = ___ 1 + 9 = ___ 3 + 10 = ___

Name ________________ Date ________________

Thinking Strategies: Switch the Order and Make 10 and Add What's Left

Show and Solve

1 Show the problem.

\+

2 Think of the answer. 3 Show the sum.

Directions Use math counters to solve each problem. Circle the larger number. Write the sum in the blank.

10 + 4 = ___	4 + 9 = ___	6 + 10 = ___	9 + 6 = ___
5 + 10 = ___	9 + 5 = ___	4 + 10 = ___	9 + 4 = ___
6 + 9 = ___	10 + 3 = ___	5 + 9 = ___	10 + 5 = ___

Name ______________________ Date ______________

Fast Facts 39

Sums 11 to 20

The activity coordinates with page 89.

10 + 6 = ___ 9 + 6 = ___

4 + 9 = ___ 4 + 10 = ___

6 + 10 = ___ 5 + 9 = ___

6 + 9 = ___ 9 + 4 = ___ 10 + 4 = ___

10 + 5 = ___ 5 + 10 = ___ 9 + 5 = ___

Name ______________________ Date ______________

Fast Facts 40

Sums 11 to 20

The activity coordinates with page 89.

6 + 9 = ___ 4 + 10 = ___

6 + 10 = ___ 9 + 6 = ___

4 + 9 = ___ 10 + 6 = ___

9 + 4 = ___ 10 + 4 = ___ 5 + 9 = ___

10 + 5 = ___ 9 + 5 = ___ 5 + 10 = ___

Name ______________________ Date ______________

Quick Check A

Sums 11 to 20

The test is on facts from pages 87–90 and previously learned facts. Alternate it with Quick Check B.

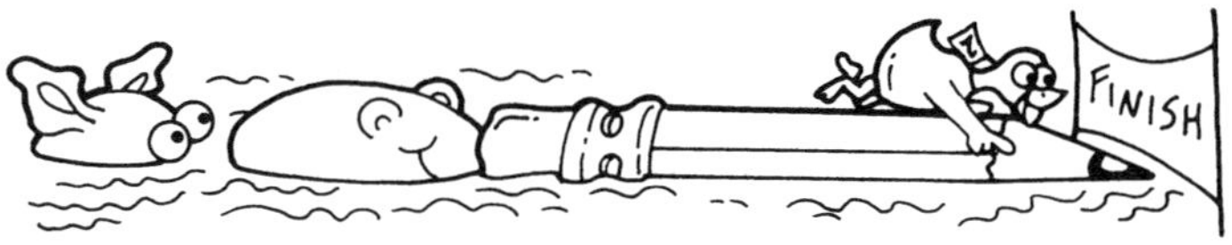

Score: __________

Time:

A	10 + 4	3 + 4	9 + 3	5 + 5	1 + 10	6 + 9
B	2 + 9	3 + 5	10 + 3	7 + 2	9 + 4	5 + 10
C	9 + 5	2 + 10	5 + 4	10 + 6	2 + 5	3 + 9
D	4 + 10	3 + 6	10 + 1	9 + 2	4 + 4	5 + 9
E	8 + 2	6 + 10	9 + 1	4 + 9	10 + 2	6 + 4
F	9 + 6	3 + 2	10 + 5	1 + 9	3 + 3	3 + 10

Name ______________________________ Date ____________________

Quick Check B

Sums 11 to 20

The test is on facts from pages 87–90 and previously learned facts. Alternate it with Quick Check B.

Score: __________

Time:

A	6 + 9	10 + 3	4 + 2	5 + 10	3 + 5	9 + 6
B	0 + 0	6 + 3	1 + 9	5 + 2	9 + 3	2 + 10
C	4 + 9	10 + 5	2 + 8	3 + 10	2 + 4	9 + 1
D	7 + 3	9 + 2	10 + 4	1 + 10	4 + 5	5 + 9
E	3 + 9	10 + 1	1 + 5	9 + 4	6 + 10	7 + 2
F	10 + 2	4 + 6	9 + 5	6 + 2	2 + 9	4 + 10

Name ______________________ Date ______________

Show and Solve

Thinking Strategies: Switch the Order and Make 10 and Add What's Left

1. Show the problem.

\+

2. Think of the answer.
3. Show the sum.

Directions Use math counters to solve each problem. Circle the larger number. Write the sum in the blank.

10 + 9 = ____	9 + 9 = ____	7 + 10 = ____	9 + 7 = ____
8 + 10 = ____	9 + 8 = ____	9 + 10 = ____	10 + 10 = ____
10 + 7 = ____	7 + 9 = ____	10 + 8 = ____	8 + 9 = ____

Name ______________________ Date ______________

Fast Facts 41

Sums 11 to 20

The activity coordinates with page 93.

10 + 10 = ___ 9 + 9 = ___

10 + 7 = ___ 9 + 7 = ___

8 + 10 = ___ 10 + 8 = ___

7 + 9 = ___ 9 + 8 = ___ 8 + 9 = ___

10 + 9 = ___ 9 + 10 = ___ 7 + 10 = ___

Name ______________________ Date ______________

Fast Facts 42

Sums 11 to 20

The activity coordinates with page 93.

8 + 9 = ___ 9 + 7 = ___

9 + 10 = ___ 10 + 10 = ___

10 + 8 = ___ 10 + 7 = ___

9 + 9 = ___ 7 + 9 = ___ 8 + 10 = ___

7 + 10 = ___ 9 + 8 = ___ 10 + 9 = ___

Partner Game—Cross the Moat

Getting Ready: Make two copies of the game cards below and the game board on page 96 on colorful card stock. Cut out the game pieces along the dashed lines. Provide 12–14 identical game markers for each player.

Playing the Game: Place the game board in the center of the playing area. Have the players decide if they should move four or six markers into the castle to win the game. Give each player a set of game markers. Sort the game cards into two piles and place them facedown near the game board. Player A draws a card from each pile and adds the numbers. The player then places a game marker on the corresponding sum. Player B continues the game in the same manner. When a player has covered two adjacent sums, those markers are moved into the castle. The first player to move the predetermined number of game markers into the castle is the winner.

Cross the Moat

11	12
13	14
15	16
17	18
19	20

11	12
13	14
15	16
17	18
19	20

Name ______________________ Date ______________

Quick Check C

Sums 11 to 20

The test is on facts from page 93 and previously learned facts. Alternate it with Quick Check D.

Score: ______

Time:

A	10 + 10	9 + 1	3 + 6	8 + 9	2 + 6	9 + 10
B	2 + 8	10 + 8	6 + 9	3 + 10	5 + 1	10 + 6
C	6 + 4	9 + 9	5 + 10	8 + 1	2 + 9	7 + 10
D	9 + 5	2 + 4	7 + 9	1 + 10	10 + 9	3 + 2
E	9 + 8	0 + 10	4 + 9	10 + 7	3 + 2	10 + 2
F	9 + 3	8 + 10	5 + 3	9 + 7	4 + 4	10 + 4

Name ____________________ Date ____________________

Quick Check D

Sums 11 to 20

The test is on facts from page 93 and previously learned facts.
Alternate it with Quick Check C.

Score: __________

Time:

A	9 + 9	3 + 4	7 + 10	1 + 8	3 + 9	4 + 10
B	10 + 1	9 + 10	6 + 3	9 + 7	0 + 6	9 + 4
C	10 + 7	3 + 7	9 + 8	5 + 9	6 + 1	2 + 10
D	10 + 3	7 + 9	1 + 10	10 + 8	5 + 4	9 + 6
E	9 + 2	1 + 7	10 + 9	3 + 5	10 + 5	8 + 9
F	10 + 10	2 + 6	1 + 9	8 + 10	0 + 9	6 + 10

Think and Solve

Thinking Strategies: Doubles, Doubles Less 1, and Doubles Plus 1

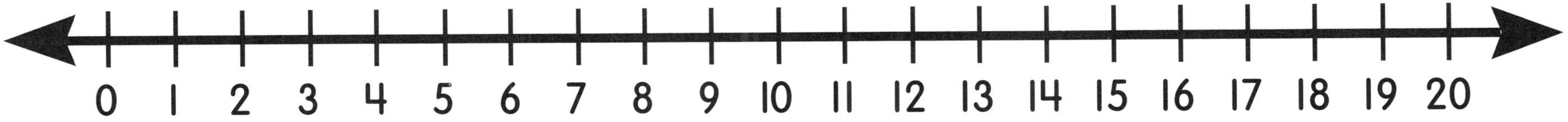

Fold on line.

Directions

- Hide the number line by folding over the top of this paper.
- Work with a partner.
- Read each problem. Then, tell your partner how you will solve it.
- Write the answer in the blank.
- Use the number line to check your answers.

5 + 5 = ___	5 + 6 = ___	6 + 6 = ___	6 + 5 = ___	6 + 7 = ___
7 + 7 = ___	7 + 8 = ___	7 + 6 = ___	8 + 8 = ___	8 + 9 = ___
8 + 7 = ___	9 + 9 = ___	9 + 10 = ___	9 + 8 = ___	

Name ________________________ Date ______________

Fast Facts 43

Sums 11 to 20

The activity coordinates with page 99.

6 + 6 = ___ 7 + 8 = ___

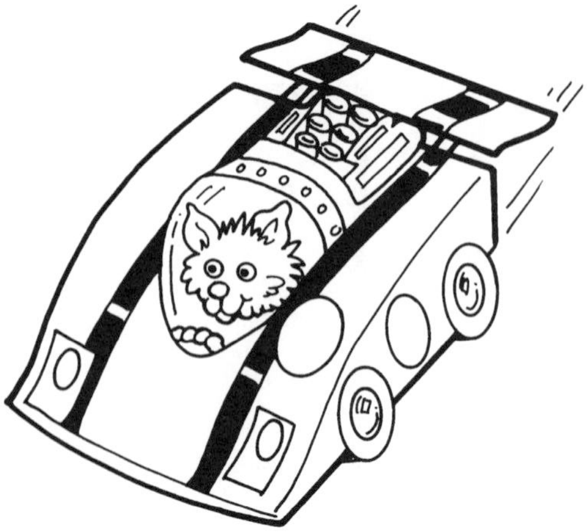

6 + 7 = ___ 8 + 9 = ___

9 + 8 = ___ 7 + 7 = ___

6 + 5 = ___ 8 + 7 = ___ 7 + 6 = ___

9 + 10 = ___ 5 + 6 = ___ 9 + 9 = ___

Name ________________________ Date ______________

Fast Facts 44

Sums 11 to 20

The activity coordinates with page 99.

7 + 8 = ___ 6 + 5 = ___

5 + 6 = ___ 9 + 8 = ___

7 + 7 = ___ 6 + 7 = ___

8 + 8 = ___ 8 + 7 = ___ 9 + 9 = ___

6 + 6 = ___ 8 + 9 = ___ 7 + 6 = ___

Name ______________________ Date ______________

Fast Facts 45

Sums 11 to 20

The activity provides more practice on new facts and coordinates with pages 99 and 100.

9 + 9 = ___ 9 + 10 = ___

5 + 6 = ___ 7 + 6 = ___

6 + 7 = ___ 8 + 9 = ___

9 + 8 = ___ 8 + 7 = ___ 8 + 8 = ___

6 + 6 = ___ 6 + 5 = ___ 7 + 8 = ___

Name ______________________ Date ______________

Fast Facts 46

Sums 11 to 20

The activity provides more practice on new facts and coordinates with pages 99 and 100.

7 + 8 = ___ 5 + 6 = ___

9 + 9 = ___ 8 + 7 = ___

7 + 7 = ___ 6 + 5 = ___

6 + 6 = ___ 9 + 8 = ___ 8 + 8 = ___

8 + 9 = ___ 7 + 6 = ___ 6 + 7 = ___

Double Smart

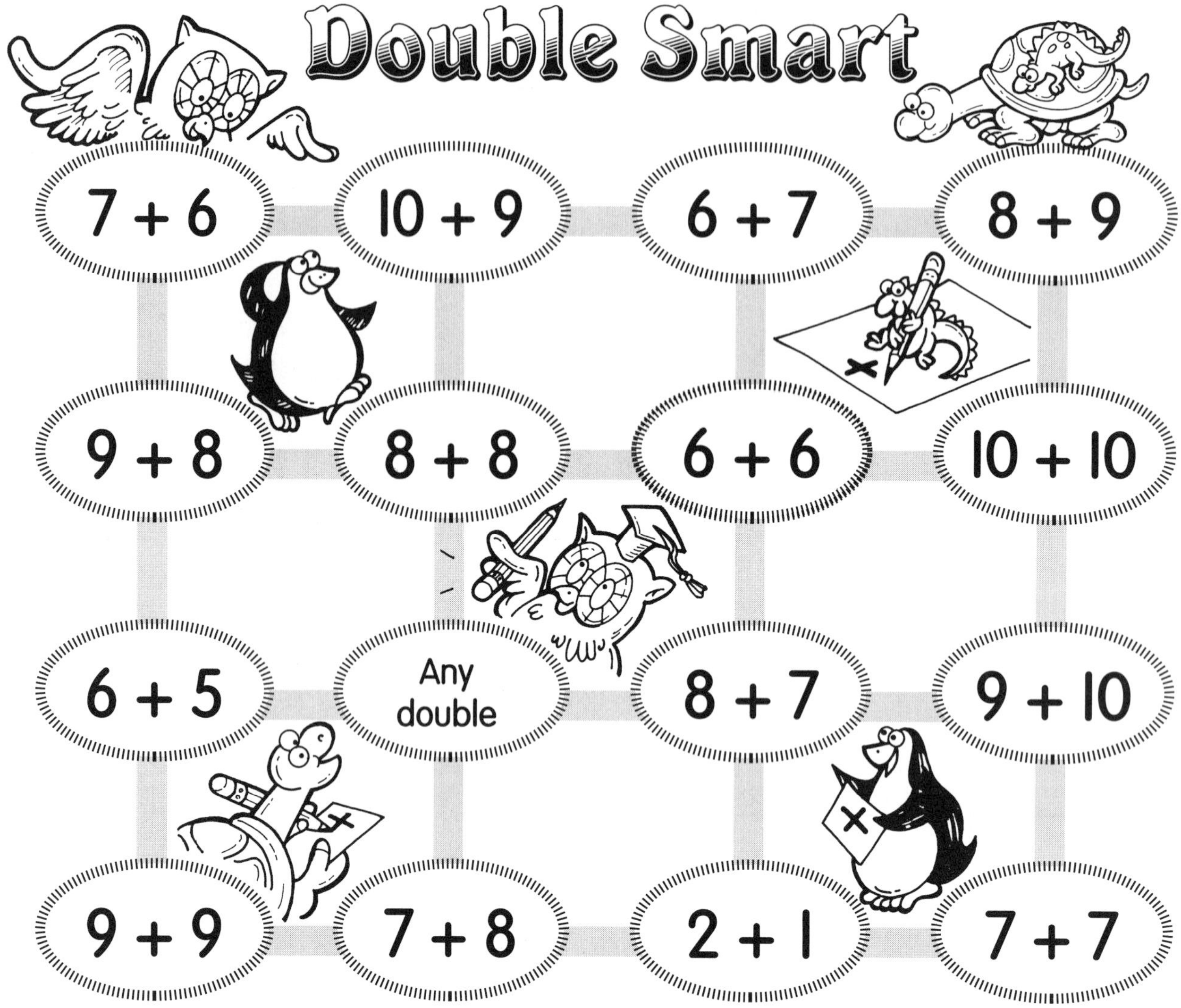

Partner Game—Double Smart

Getting Ready: Copy the game board on this page and the dice on page 103 onto colorful card stock. Cut out the game pieces along the dashed lines. To form each die, fold along the solid lines to make the cube shape and then glue the tabs as indicated under the numerals. Provide 10 identical game markers for each player.

Playing the Game: Give each player a set of game markers. Place the game board in the center of the playing area. To begin the game, Player A rolls both dies and then adds the numbers together. The player must *say the math sentence correctly out loud* and then look for the corresponding problem on the game board. Player B should listen carefully to catch any errors. For example, if 6 + 6 and + 1 are rolled, Player A says, "6 + 6 + 1 is the same as 6 + 7 = 13." Player A covers the correct fact (6 + 7) on the game board. (The first number in the fact establishes the double for comparison.) If the fact has already been covered or if Player A does not verbalize the math sentence correctly, Player A 's turn is over. Player B then takes a turn. If the words "Any double" are rolled, the player chooses which double to use to make the math fact. To cover the words "Any double" on the game board, the player must roll a double and + 0. The game ends when one player covers four spaces in a vertical, horizontal or diagonal row. Otherwise, the player who covers the most spaces wins the game.

Doubles Die

Glue here.

9 + 9

Any double

6 + 6

8 + 8

10 + 10

Glue here.

Glue here.

7 + 7

Addend Die

Glue here.

+1

+0

−1

+0

−1

Glue here.

Glue here.

+1

Name ______________________ Date ______________

Quick Check E

Sums 11 to 20

The test is on facts from pages 99–101 and previously learned facts. Alternate it with Quick Check F.

Score: ________

Time:

A	8 + 8	7 + 9	2 + 5	6 + 10	9 + 2	5 + 4
B	7 + 10	6 + 5	8 + 9	3 + 6	7 + 7	9 + 6
C	10 + 7	9 + 9	3 + 0	5 + 6	4 + 1	9 + 8
D	5 + 9	7 + 8	2 + 7	10 + 10	4 + 6	5 + 5
E	1 + 9	5 + 3	6 + 6	10 + 8	9 + 4	8 + 7
F	7 + 6	3 + 9	7 + 0	4 + 5	6 + 7	9 + 10

Name ______________________ Date ______________

Quick Check F

Sums 11 to 20

The test is on facts from pages 99–101 and previously learned facts. Alternate it with Quick Check E.

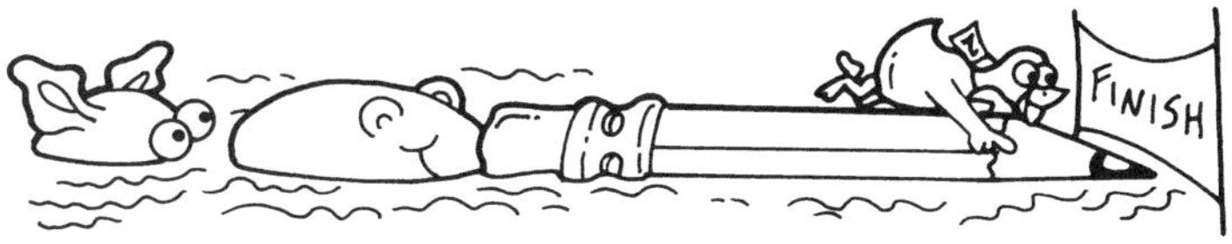

Score: ________

Time:

A	7 + 7	8 + 10	7 + 3	8 + 9	1 + 3	9 + 1
B	10 + 5	8 + 7	5 + 5	9 + 7	0 + 8	6 + 7
C	5 + 4	7 + 1	9 + 10	8 + 8	4 + 3	7 + 8
D	4 + 9	9 + 9	2 + 3	9 + 5	0 + 5	5 + 6
E	9 + 8	3 + 5	10 + 10	2 + 9	7 + 6	6 + 9
F	6 + 5	9 + 3	4 + 6	7 + 2	6 + 6	10 + 9

Name ____________________ Date ____________

Thinking Strategies: Switch the Order and Make 10 and Add What's Left

Show and Solve

1 Show the problem.

+

2 Think of the answer.

3 Show the sum.

Directions Use math counters to solve each problem.
Circle the larger number. Write the sum in the blank.

8 + 2 = ___ 4 + 8 = ___ 8 + 6 = ___ 3 + 8 = ___ 8 + 5 = ___

5 + 8 = ___ 8 + 3 = ___ 2 + 8 = ___ 8 + 4 = ___ 6 + 8 = ___

Name ______________________________ Date ______________

Fast Facts 47

Sums 11 to 20

The activity coordinates with page 106 and includes two previously learned facts.

2 + 8 = ____ 5 + 8 = ____

6 + 8 = ____ 3 + 8 = ____

4 + 8 = ____ 8 + 2 = ____

8 + 5 = ____ 5 + 5 = ____ 8 + 4 = ____

5 + 6 = ____ 8 + 3 = ____ 8 + 6 = ____

Name ______________________________ Date ______________

Fast Facts 48

Sums 11 to 20

The activity coordinates with page 106 and includes two previously learned facts.

8 + 2 = ____ 5 + 8 = ____

8 + 6 = ____ 3 + 8 = ____

5 + 6 = ____ 8 + 4 = ____

8 + 3 = ____ 4 + 8 = ____ 8 + 5 = ____

6 + 8 = ____ 5 + 5 = ____ 2 + 8 = ____

Name ______________________ Date ______________

Quick Check G

Sums 11 to 20

The test is on facts from page 106 and previously learned facts. Alternate it with Quick Check H.

Score: ________

Time:

A	5 + 8	9 + 3	8 + 2	7 + 7	8 + 9	3 + 3
B	10 + 9	6 + 8	2 + 9	6 + 4	8 + 3	7 + 8
C	8 + 4	4 + 10	5 + 5	3 + 9	6 + 5	9 + 8
D	6 + 6	8 + 6	7 + 10	4 + 8	5 + 3	8 + 7
E	5 + 9	8 + 5	4 + 4	3 + 8	5 + 10	9 + 9
F	8 + 10	4 + 9	2 + 8	7 + 6	6 + 3	8 + 8

Name ______________________________ Date __________________

Quick Check H

Sums 11 to 20

The test is on facts from page 106 and previously learned facts. Alternate it with Quick Check G.

Score: ____________

Time:

A	8 + 7	3 + 8	9 + 0	8 + 5	6 + 5	9 + 2
B	9 + 6	6 + 6	8 + 9	3 + 4	2 + 8	9 + 4
C	7 + 6	10 + 2	4 + 8	7 + 3	8 + 8	6 + 10
D	8 + 2	6 + 7	9 + 9	4 + 6	5 + 8	9 + 5
E	9 + 8	8 + 4	3 + 6	7 + 8	9 + 10	8 + 6
F	6 + 8	4 + 5	5 + 6	8 + 3	7 + 7	10 + 3

Show and Solve

Thinking Strategies: Switch the Order and Make 10 and Add What's Left

1 Show the problem.

+

2 Think of the answer. 3 Show the sum.

Directions Use math counters to solve each problem.
Circle the larger number. Write the sum in the blank.

3 + 7 = ___ 7 + 6 = ___ 7 + 3 = ___ 4 + 7 = ___ 7 + 5 = ___

7 + 4 = ___ 5 + 7 = ___ 7 + 7 = ___ 6 + 7 = ___ 8 + 7 = ___

Name ______________________ Date ______________

Fast Facts 49

Sums 11 to 20

The activity coordinates with page 110 and includes a few previously learned facts.

$7 + 4 =$ ___ $4 + 7 =$ ___

$7 + 7 =$ ___ $7 + 6 =$ ___

$8 + 7 =$ ___ $7 + 3 =$ ___

$7 + 5 =$ ___ $5 + 7 =$ ___ $6 + 7 =$ ___

$8 + 8 =$ ___ $7 + 8 =$ ___ $3 + 7 =$ ___

Name ______________________ Date ______________

Fast Facts 50

Sums 11 to 20

The activity coordinates with page 110 and includes a few previously learned facts.

$7 + 6 =$ ___ $6 + 6 =$ ___

$3 + 7 =$ ___ $4 + 7 =$ ___

$7 + 4 =$ ___ $7 + 5 =$ ___

$7 + 8 =$ ___ $7 + 7 =$ ___ $6 + 7 =$ ___

$5 + 7 =$ ___ $8 + 7 =$ ___ $7 + 3 =$ ___

Addend Die

Glue here.

Choose any plane.

8 +

7 +

8 +

7 +

Glue here.

Glue here.

Return to hangar.

Partner Game—Number Soar

Getting Ready: Make three copies of the game cards below, one copy of the die above, and one copy of page 113 on colorful card stock. Cut out the game pieces along the dashed lines. To form the die, fold along the solid lines to make the cube shape and then glue the tabs as indicated. Provide 10–12 identical markers for each player.

Playing the Game: To begin the game, place the game board in the center of the playing area. Give each player a set of game markers. Shuffle the cards and place them facedown in a pile. Player A rolls the die, draws a card, verbalizes the addition sentence, and then covers the correct sum displayed on an airplane. Player B should listen carefully for errors. If the number is already covered or if the sum is incorrect, Player A's turn is over. Player B then continues the game in the same manner. When the words "Return to hangar" are rolled, one of the player's game pieces must be removed from the game board. For the words, "Choose any plane," the player chooses one airplane and covers it with a game marker. The first player to cover four adjacent airplanes is declared the winner.

3	5	7	9
2	4	6	8

Make three copies.

Number Soar

Cover four planes in a row to win!

Name ____________________ Date ____________________

Quick Check I

Sums 11 to 20

The test is on facts from page 110 and previously learned facts. Alternate it with Quick Check J. The new facts are repeated for extra practice.

Score: ________

Time:

A	5 + 7	9 + 9	3 + 10	4 + 8	7 + 4	8 + 7
B	10 + 4	7 + 4	6 + 5	9 + 8	3 + 8	7 + 6
C	8 + 5	6 + 6	7 + 5	9 + 7	6 + 7	9 + 4
D	4 + 7	7 + 7	10 + 6	4 + 7	7 + 9	8 + 3
E	5 + 6	8 + 4	7 + 5	2 + 10	6 + 8	9 + 6
F	8 + 10	5 + 8	8 + 8	8 + 6	5 + 7	7 + 8

Name ______________________________ Date ____________________

Quick Check J

Sums 11 to 20

The test is on facts from page 110 and previously learned facts. Alternate it with Quick Check I. The new facts are repeated for extra practice.

Score: ____________

Time:

A	7 + 4	5 + 9	7 + 7	9 + 10	5 + 7	6 + 9
B	4 + 9	7 + 5	9 + 7	4 + 7	7 + 10	6 + 5
C	9 + 8	7 + 4	8 + 3	7 + 6	8 + 8	5 + 8
D	5 + 10	8 + 4	5 + 6	6 + 8	5 + 7	9 + 3
E	3 + 8	7 + 8	4 + 7	8 + 5	10 + 10	8 + 9
F	2 + 9	6 + 7	4 + 8	9 + 5	7 + 5	8 + 6

Name ______________________ Date ______________

50 Nifty Facts A

Sums 11 to 20

Alternate this test with page 117.

A	3 + 8	9 + 9	7 + 10	4 + 7	6 + 10
B	8 + 5	6 + 5	10 + 4	8 + 7	3 + 9
C	4 + 10	7 + 4	8 + 4	8 + 9	7 + 7
D	6 + 7	4 + 9	9 + 2	5 + 7	6 + 6
E	7 + 5	5 + 10	10 + 7	5 + 8	6 + 9
F	8 + 8	5 + 9	7 + 6	9 + 4	10 + 1
G	10 + 10	10 + 5	9 + 7	2 + 10	8 + 6
H	8 + 3	9 + 6	5 + 6	9 + 3	10 + 9
I	9 + 5	10 + 3	7 + 9	6 + 8	4 + 8
J	3 + 10	2 + 9	8 + 10	7 + 8	9 + 8

Name ______________________ Date ______________

50 Nifty Facts B

Sums 11 to 20

Alternate this test with page 116.

A	10 + 2	7 + 7	8 + 4	5 + 6	9 + 8
B	9 + 10	4 + 7	9 + 9	7 + 6	10 + 1
C	9 + 5	2 + 10	5 + 7	2 + 9	5 + 8
D	10 + 8	4 + 8	6 + 9	10 + 10	4 + 9
E	7 + 5	9 + 7	6 + 6	8 + 3	7 + 8
F	8 + 8	6 + 8	3 + 9	7 + 4	8 + 9
G	3 + 8	10 + 9	8 + 7	9 + 6	6 + 7
H	7 + 9	6 + 5	9 + 4	10 + 6	8 + 5
I	6 + 10	10 + 3	7 + 10	5 + 9	9 + 2
J	4 + 10	9 + 3	10 + 5	8 + 6	1 + 10

Think and Solve

Thinking Strategies: How Far Apart?
Count Up and Count Back

0 1 2 3 4 5 6 7 8 9 10 11 12 13 14 15 16 17 18 19 20

Fold on line.

Directions

- Hide the number line by folding over the top of this paper.
- Work with a partner.
- Read each problem. Then, tell your partner how you will solve it.
- Write the answer in the blank.
- Use the number line to check your answers.

A	B	C	D	E
9 + ___ = 12	3 + ___ = 11	10 + ___ = 13	14 + ___ = 14	3 + ___ = 12
___ + 18 = 18	___ + 10 = 12	___ + 9 = 12	9 + ___ = 11	___ + 8 = 11
3 + ___ = 13	___ + 2 = 11	16 + ___ = 16	___ + 2 = 12	2 + ___ = 11

Name ______________________ Date ______________

Fast Facts 51

Sums 11 to 20

The activity coordinates with page 118.

2 + ___ = 12   ___ + 9 = 11

3 + ___ = 11   3 + ___ = 12

11 + ___ = 11   8 + ___ = 11

___ + 3 = 12   ___ + 19 = 19   0 + ___ = 17

10 + ___ = 13   ___ + 14 = 14   2 + ___ = 11

Name ______________________ Date ______________

Fast Facts 52

Sums 11 to 20

The activity coordinates with page 118.

9 + ___ = 11   12 + ___ = 12

___ + 3 = 12   1 + ___ = 11

0 + ___ = 13   ___ + 3 = 11

___ + 8 = 11   ___ + 15 = 15   3 + ___ = 13

10 + ___ = 11   10 + ___ = 12   ___ + 2 = 11

Think and Solve

Thinking Strategies: How Far Apart? Count Up and Count Back and Make 10—How Much More Is Needed?

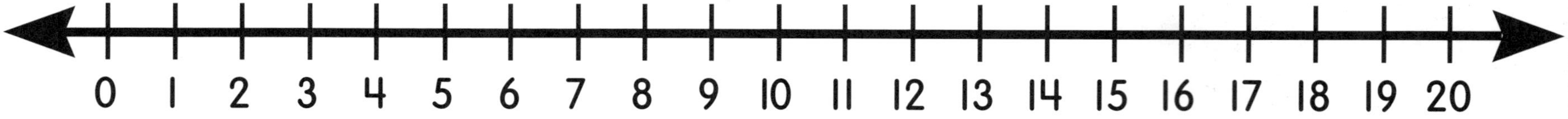

Fold on line.

Directions

- Hide the number line by folding over the top of this paper.
- Work with a partner.
- Read each problem. Then, tell your partner how you will solve it.
- Write the answer in the blank.
- Use the number line to check your answers.

A	B	C	D	E
9 + ____ = 14	____ + 5 = 12	____ + 10 = 15	5 + ____ = 13	7 + ____ = 11
____ + 4 = 12	____ + 9 = 13	____ + 7 = 12	____ + 10 = 14	____ + 9 = 14
____ + 5 = 15	8 + ____ = 13	10 + ____ = 14	9 + ____ = 13	____ + 8 = 12

Name ______________________ Date ______________

Fast Facts 53 Sums 11 to 20

The activity coordinates with page 120.

___ + 5 = 15   ___ + 9 = 13

8 + ___ = 13   ___ + 4 = 12

___ + 7 = 11   7 + ___ = 12

10 + ___ = 14   ___ + 9 = 14   5 + ___ = 13

___ + 4 = 13   7 + ___ = 11   ___ + 8 = 12

Name ______________________ Date ______________

Fast Facts 54 Sums 11 to 20

The activity coordinates with page 120.

5 + ___ = 12   10 + ___ = 15

___ + 4 = 13   7 + ___ = 12

4 + ___ = 11   ___ + 8 = 13

___ + 4 = 11   5 + ___ = 14   4 + ___ = 14

4 + ___ = 13   ___ + 5 = 13   ___ + 8 = 12

Name ______________________ Date ______________

Think and Write

Sums 11 to 20

The activity coordinates with pages 118–121.

___ + 9 = 11 ___ + 0 = 14

___ + 5 = 12 5 + ___ = 14

5 + ___ = 15 ___ + 2 = 11 9 + ___ = 13

___ + 9 = 12 ___ + 5 = 13 ___ + 7 = 11

---

11 + 0 = ___ ___ = 5 + 8 ___ = 0 + 17

4 + 10 = ___ 9 + 3 = ___ 10 + 5 = ___

___ = 2 + 9 ___ = 5 + 7 ___ = 7 + 4

___ = 8 + 4 20 + 0 = ___ ___ = 5 + 9

___ + 4 = 13 ___ + 14 = 14 ___ + 5 = 13

10 + ___ = 11 4 + ___ = 11 ___ + 2 = 12

8 + ___ = 12 10 + ___ = 15 ___ + 8 = 11

___ + 10 = 13 ___ + 3 = 12 7 + ___ = 12

Name ____________ Date ____________

Think and Solve

Thinking Strategy: Make 10—How Much More Is Needed?

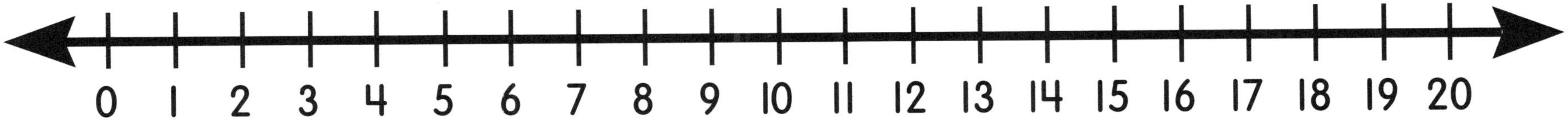

Fold on line.

Directions

- Hide the number line by folding over the top of this paper.
- Work with a partner.
- Read each problem. Then, tell your partner how you will solve it.
- Write the answer in the blank.
- Use the number line to check your answers.

A	B	C	D	E
___ + 8 = 18	9 + ___ = 15	7 + ___ = 15	10 + ___ = 18	6 + ___ = 15
6 + ___ = 14	___ + 7 = 15	___ + 7 = 16	___ + 10 = 16	8 + ___ = 14
___ + 9 = 15	___ + 9 = 16	10 + ___ = 17	7 + ___ = 17	6 + ___ = 16

Name ______________________ Date ______________

Fast Facts 55

Sums 11 to 20

The activity coordinates with page 123.

___ + 6 = 15   ___ + 8 = 18

___ + 10 = 18   ___ + 8 = 15

___ + 9 = 15   7 + ___ = 16

8 + ___ = 15   ___ + 6 = 14   10 + ___ = 16

___ + 7 = 17   9 + ___ = 16   ___ + 8 = 14

Name ______________________ Date ______________

Fast Facts 56

Sums 11 to 20

The activity coordinates with page 123.

___ + 8 = 18   ___ + 6 = 15

7 + ___ = 15   8 + ___ = 15

9 + ___ = 16   ___ + 10 = 18

___ + 10 = 17   7 + ___ = 17   8 + ___ = 14

___ + 9 = 15   ___ + 10 = 16   ___ + 6 = 16

Think and Solve

Thinking Strategies: Doubles, Doubles Less 1, Doubles Plus 1, and Make 10—How Much More Is Needed?

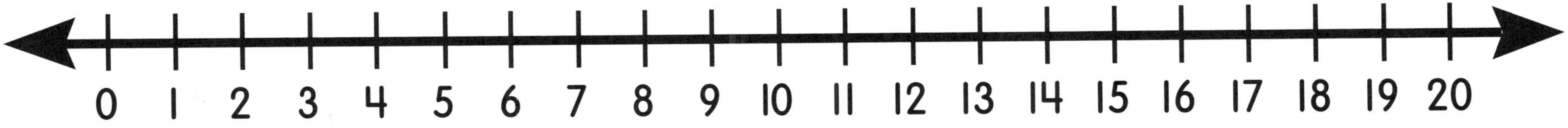

Fold on line.

Directions

- Hide the number line by folding over the top of this paper.
- Work with a partner.
- Read each problem. Then, tell your partner how you will solve it.
- Write the answer in the blank.
- Use the number line to check your answers.

A	B	C	D	E
7 + ___ = 15	6 + ___ = 12	___ + 9 = 17	___ + 9 = 18	8 + ___ = 15
___ + 10 = 20	___ + 8 = 17	6 + ___ = 13	7 + ___ = 14	5 + ___ = 11
8 + ___ = 16	___ + 5 = 11	___ + 10 = 19	___ + 9 = 19	7 + ___ = 13

Name ______________________ Date ______________

Fast Facts 57

Sums 11 to 20

The activity coordinates with page 125.

10 + ___ = 19   8 + ___ = 17

___ + 6 = 13   7 + ___ = 14

9 + ___ = 17   ___ + 6 = 12

8 + ___ = 16   ___ + 8 = 15   ___ + 5 = 11

___ + 7 = 15   ___ + 6 = 11   9 + ___ = 18

Name ______________________ Date ______________

Fast Facts 58

Sums 11 to 20

The activity coordinates with page 125.

7 + ___ = 15   6 + ___ = 12

___ + 6 = 13   8 + ___ = 17

8 + ___ = 15   5 + ___ = 11

6 + ___ = 11   ___ + 10 = 20   ___ + 8 = 16

___ + 7 = 14   6 + ___ = 13   ___ + 9 = 19

Name ______________________ Date ______________

Think and Write

Sums 11 to 20

The activity coordinates with pages 123–126.

8 + ___ = 18   ___ + 8 = 14

___ + 10 = 20   6 + ___ = 12

5 + ___ = 11   ___ + 10 = 17   ___ + 9 = 19

___ + 6 = 15   7 + ___ = 14   7 + ___ = 16

___ = 8 + 8   10 + 8 = ___   5 + 6 = ___

6 + 10 = ___   ___ = 6 + 7   ___ = 9 + 9

___ = 9 + 6   ___ = 10 + 10   10 + 7 = ___

7 + 8 = ___   8 + 9 = ___   ___ = 9 + 10

___ + 9 = 17   ___ + 9 = 18   7 + ___ = 13

6 + ___ = 16   8 + ___ = 15   ___ + 5 = 11

___ + 10 = 18   ___ + 6 = 14   7 + ___ = 16

8 + ___ = 16   6 + ___ = 15   ___ + 7 = 14

Partner Game—Missing Number Mission

Getting Ready: Copy the materials on pages 129–132 onto colorful card stock. Cut out the game pieces along the dashed lines. Trim around the game board pieces as desired and then glue them together so that the borders overlap at the center of the scene. Each orbit will be oval in shape when the scene is assembled. Provide two identical game markers or "rockets" for each player.

Playing the Game: To begin the game, place the game board in the center of the playing area. Give each player a pair of rocket game markers to set on "Earth." Shuffle the game cards and place them facedown in a pile near the game board. Player A draws a card and answers the missing addend. That player launches one rocket off Earth and moves it counterclockwise the number of spaces designated by the missing addend. For example, if the problem is 6 + _ = 13, the player moves the game marker 7 spaces on the first orbit. Player B should listen carefully for errors. If the answer is incorrect, Player A's turn is over. Player B then continues the game in the same manner. When a player's marker lands on a circle with an arrow, the player slides that rocket out to the next orbit and stops on the designated circle. Only one rocket game marker can rest on a circle. If a player lands on a circle that is covered by one of the opponent's rockets, the opponent's game marker is sent back to Earth "for repairs."

Special Rules for Moving Both Rockets During a Turn:

- Only when a player has both rockets orbiting Earth can the answer for a math fact be partitioned into 2 moves. For example, if the missing addend answer is 9, the player could split that number into 6 + 3 and then move the first rocket 6 spaces and the second rocket 3 spaces.
- When a rocket game marker lands on a circle with an arrow, the marker is slid out to the next orbit and rests on the designated circle. The remaining portion of the missing addend answer is then used by that player to move the second rocket. This strategy is effective for moving the rockets from Earth into deep space quickly.

The first player to move both of the game markers beyond the orbit paths into deep space wins the game.

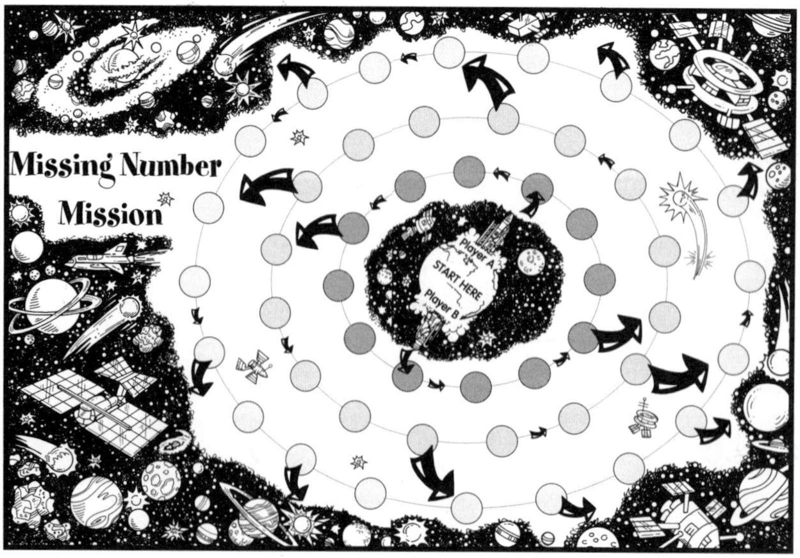

8 + ___ = 10	10 + ___ = 14	10 + ___ = 15	10 + ___ = 16	10 + ___ = 18	9 + ___ = 19
3 + ___ = 13	3 + ___ = 10	4 + ___ = 11	10 + ___ = 17	5 + ___ = 15	6 + ___ = 16
6 + ___ = 13	6 + ___ = 14	6 + ___ = 15	5 + ___ = 10	5 + ___ = 11	5 + ___ = 12
5 + ___ = 13	5 + ___ = 14	7 + ___ = 17	4 + ___ = 12	4 + ___ = 13	3 + ___ = 11
3 + ___ = 12	2 + ___ = 10	2 + ___ = 11	2 + ___ = 12	4 + ___ = 10	4 + ___ = 14

7 + ___ = 14	9 + ___ = 17	9 + ___ = 11	8 + ___ = 13	Repair your spacecraft. Lose a turn.
7 + ___ = 15	9 + ___ = 18	9 + ___ = 12	8 + ___ = 14	Repair your spacecraft. Lose a turn.
7 + ___ = 16	7 + ___ = 10	9 + ___ = 13	8 + ___ = 15	Repair your spacecraft. Lose a turn.
6 + ___ = 10	7 + ___ = 11	9 + ___ = 14	8 + ___ = 16	Repair your spacecraft. Lose a turn.
6 + ___ = 11	7 + ___ = 12	9 + ___ = 15	8 + ___ = 17	8 + ___ = 11
6 + ___ = 12	7 + ___ = 13	9 + ___ = 16	8 + ___ = 18	8 + ___ = 12

Missing Number Mission

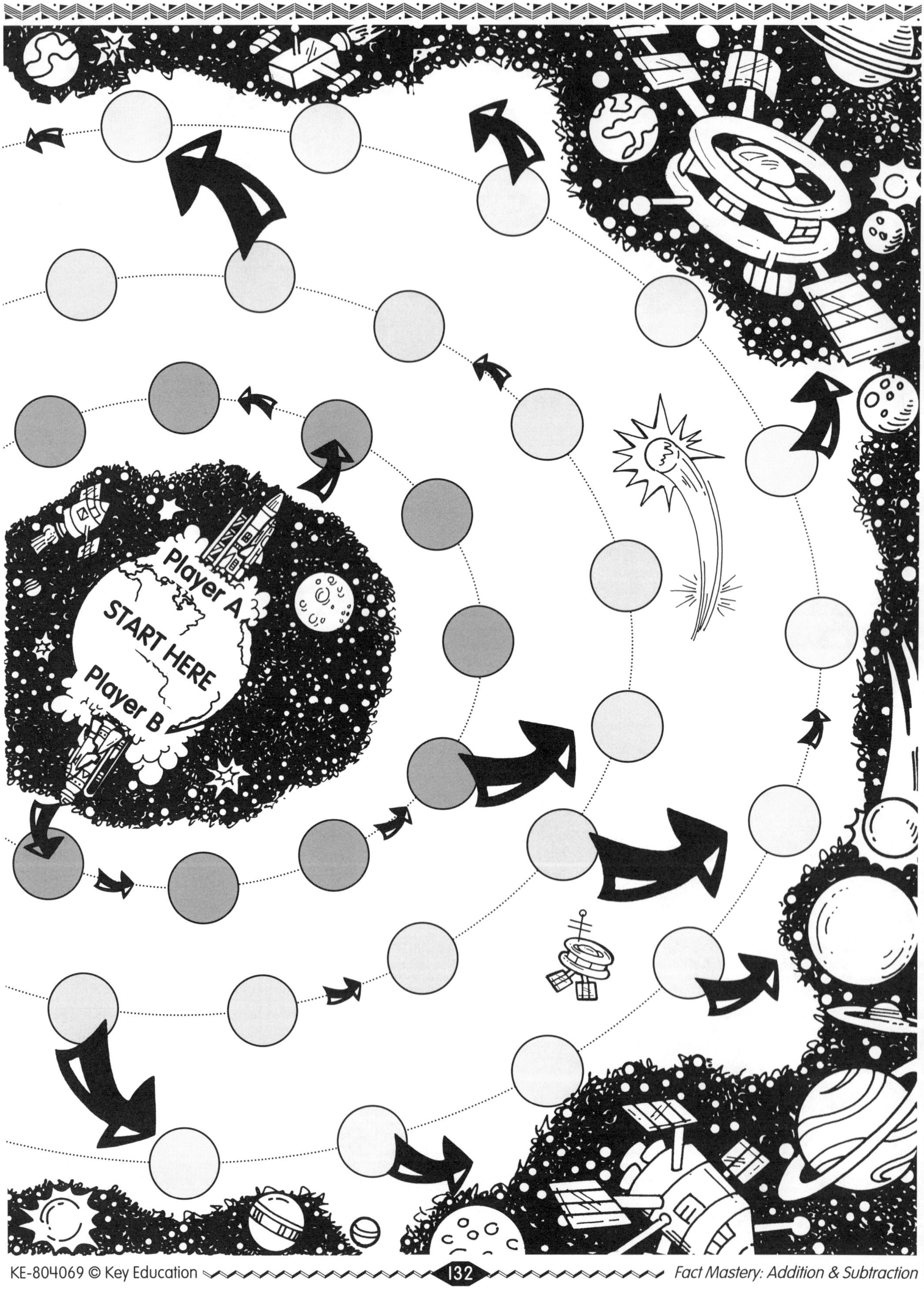
Player A
START HERE
Player B

Fact Mastery: Minuends 11 to 20

When students can quickly recall the answers for addition facts with sums from 11 to 20, challenge them with activities and timed tests for learning the related subtraction facts. As each strategy is introduced, print its name in a prominent location. Then, students may refer to the list when solving subtraction problems on the Show and Solve, Think and Solve, and Fast Facts practice pages. *To help students develop the habit of using mental strategies, it is recommended that they verbalize their methods for solving the math problems to their partners.* Point out how it is possible to calculate the answer for a problem in different ways.

Strategies to Introduce and Use

How Far Apart? Count Back. When students are subtracting a small number such as 1 , 2, or 3, have them count back from the minuend the corresponding subtrahend. To do this, ask students to make a fist to represent the minuend. Tap the fist with the other hand when saying the minuend *as if you have packed your hand with that number of counters,* and then continue by extending the corresponding number of fingers while counting back from the minuend. For example, to solve 12 – 3, make a fist, say the number 12 *(tap the fist),* and then count back 3 *(11, 10, 9—extending a finger for each number).* Finally, announce the answer as 9.

To help students internalize these number relationships and not depend on counting on their fingers or objects, provide lots of practice on the facts introduced on pages 144, 146, and 164. Pair off students and have them tell each other the answers for subtraction problems that you call out. You might also have students write the featured facts on index cards for additional practice.

Think Addition. Provide lots of practice for students to identify the related addition sentences in a fact family. Have students pair off. Call out to the class any of the subtraction problems featured on the Show and Solve, Think and Solve, and Fast Facts pages provided in this section of the book. Have students quickly verbalize the related addition facts with missing addends.

Think Addition and Make 10—How Much More Is Needed? Here is another strategy that can be used when working with subtraction problems. When calculating a subtraction problem, students can think of its related addition fact with a missing addend and then determine how much more is needed so that the addends equal the sum of the problem. For example, to solve 12 – 8, begin the process by thinking of the related addition problem 8 + ? = 12 and then use 8 + $\underline{2}$ = 10 and 10 + $\underline{2}$ = 12. The missing addend is 4 (2 + 2), which is also the difference for the related subtraction fact (12 – 8 = 4). Have students pair off for the mental math activities. Call out various subtraction problems for them to discuss and solve. Use the facts introduced on pages 136, 138, 140, 144, 146, 150, 156, 158, and 164. You might also have students write the featured facts on index cards for additional practice.

Think Addition and Use Double Facts. When students know the double facts, it is easy for them to apply that knowledge to solve other subtraction problems. Demonstrate this strategy by using the related double facts for corresponding subtraction problems. For example, to solve 16 – 8, think 8 + 8 = 16 to calculate that the difference would be 8. Continue the exercise by constructing mental comparisons with addends that are 1 less or 1 more than one of the addends of the double fact. For example, to solve 16 – 7, think of the double fact 8 + 8 = 16. By comparing this double fact with 7 + ? = 16, the student now knows that the difference is the double (8) plus 1, or 9. (To calculate the answer, think of 7 as 1 less than 8. Then, add the extra 1 to the second 8.) Pair off students. Call out math facts from page 150 and have students discuss and solve the problems. You might also have students write the featured facts on index cards for independent study.

Name ______________________ Date ______________

Pretest/Posttest

Score: ________

A	20 − 10	13 − 4	16 − 9	11 − 6	13 − 7	11 − 8	17 − 10
B	12 − 3	13 − 8	11 − 7	14 − 6	18 − 8	12 − 5	11 − 9
C	15 − 5	11 − 2	14 − 8	13 − 9	12 − 4	14 − 10	16 − 7
D	13 − 5	12 − 8	15 − 6	12 − 7	15 − 9	11 − 3	14 − 4
E	14 − 7	11 − 4	17 − 7	12 − 6	18 − 9	13 − 10	15 − 8
F	12 − 9	16 − 6	14 − 5	17 − 9	16 − 8	11 − 5	18 − 10
G	13 − 6	12 − 2	14 − 9	15 − 7	17 − 8	12 − 10	19 − 9

Progress Chart

Minuends 11 to 20

Name	Quick Check A	Quick Check B	Quick Check C	Quick Check D	Quick Check E	Quick Check F	Quick Check G	Quick Check H	50 Facts A	50 Facts B

Name ____________ Date ____________

Think and Solve

Thinking Strategy: Think Addition and Make 10—How Much More Is Needed?

0 1 2 3 4 5 6 7 8 9 10 11 12 13 14 15 16 17 18 19 20

Fold on line.

Directions

- Hide the number line by folding over the top of this paper.
- Work with a partner.
- Read each problem. Then, tell your partner how you will solve it.
- Write the answer in the blank.
- Use the number line to check your answers.

11 − 10 = ____   10 + ____ = 11   12 − 10 = ____   10 + ____ = 12

11 − 9 = ____   9 + ____ = 11   12 − 9 = ____   9 + ____ = 12

13 − 10 = ____   10 + ____ = 13   13 − 9 = ____   9 + ____ = 13

Name ______________________ Date ______________

Fast Facts 59

Minuends 11 to 20

The activity coordinates with page 136.

10 + ___ = 12 12 − 10 = ___

9 + ___ = 11 11 − 9 = ___

11 − 10 = ___ 13 − 10 = ___

12 − 9 = ___ 10 + ___ = 11 10 + ___ = 13

9 + ___ = 13 13 − 9 = ___ 9 + ___ = 12

Name ______________________ Date ______________

Fast Facts 60

Minuends 11 to 20

The activity coordinates with page 136.

9 + ___ = 13 10 + ___ = 12

12 − 10 = ___ 11 − 9 = ___

9 + ___ = 11 10 + ___ = 13

13 − 9 = ___ 10 + ___ = 11 9 + ___ = 12

11 − 10 = ___ 12 − 9 = ___ 13 − 10 = ___

Name ____________________ Date ____________________

Think and Solve

Thinking Strategy: Think Addition and Make 10—How Much More Is Needed?

0 1 2 3 4 5 6 7 8 9 10 11 12 13 14 15 16 17 18 19 20

Fold on line.

Directions

- Hide the number line by folding over the top of this paper.
- Work with a partner.
- Read each problem. Then, tell your partner how you will solve it.
- Write the answer in the blank.
- Use the number line to check your answers.

15 − 10 = ____ 10 + ____ = 15 14 − 10 = ____ 10 + ____ = 14

16 − 9 = ____ 9 + ____ = 16 15 − 9 = ____ 9 + ____ = 15

16 − 10 = ____ 10 + ____ = 16 14 − 9 = ____ 9 + ____ = 14

Name ______________________ Date ______________

Fast Facts 61

Minuends 11 to 20

The activity coordinates with page 138.

16 − 9 = ___

10 + ___ = 15

9 + ___ = 16

14 − 9 = ___

15 − 10 = ___

14 − 10 = ___

16 − 10 = ___

10 + ___ = 14

10 + ___ = 16

9 + ___ = 14

15 − 9 = ___

9 + ___ = 15

Name ______________________ Date ______________

Fast Facts 62

Minuends 11 to 20

The activity coordinates with page 138.

10 + ___ = 16

9 + ___ = 16

15 − 9 = ___

14 − 9 = ___

9 + ___ = 15

10 + ___ = 15

14 − 10 = ___

10 + ___ = 14

9 + ___ = 14

16 − 10 = ___

16 − 9 = ___

15 − 10 = ___

Think and Solve

Thinking Strategy: Think Addition and Make 10—How Much More Is Needed?

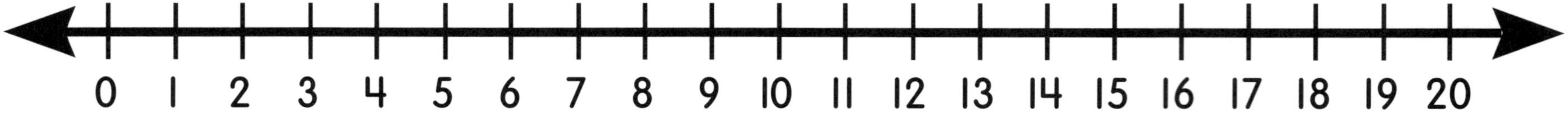

Fold on line.

Directions

- Hide the number line by folding over the top of this paper.
- Work with a partner.
- Read each problem. Then, tell your partner how you will solve it.
- Write the answer in the blank.
- Use the number line to check your answers.

20 − 10 = ___   10 + ___ = 20   18 − 10 = ___   10 + ___ = 18

17 − 9 = ___   9 + ___ = 17   19 − 10 = ___   10 + ___ = 19

17 − 10 = ___   10 + ___ = 17   18 − 9 = ___   9 + ___ = 18

Name ____________________ Date ____________

Fast Facts 63

Minuends 11 to 20

The activity coordinates with page 140.

$17 - 10 = \underline{\hspace{2em}}$ $10 + \underline{\hspace{2em}} = 20$

$9 + \underline{\hspace{2em}} = 19$ $18 - 9 = \underline{\hspace{2em}}$

$20 - 10 = \underline{\hspace{2em}}$ $19 - 10 = \underline{\hspace{2em}}$

$18 - 10 = \underline{\hspace{2em}}$ $10 + \underline{\hspace{2em}} = 18$ $10 + \underline{\hspace{2em}} = 17$

$9 + \underline{\hspace{2em}} = 17$ $17 - 9 = \underline{\hspace{2em}}$ $19 - 9 = \underline{\hspace{2em}}$

Name ____________________ Date ____________

Fast Facts 64

Minuends 11 to 20

The activity coordinates with page 140.

$10 + \underline{\hspace{2em}} = 19$ $9 + \underline{\hspace{2em}} = 17$

$20 - 10 = \underline{\hspace{2em}}$ $17 - 10 = \underline{\hspace{2em}}$

$9 + \underline{\hspace{2em}} = 18$ $10 + \underline{\hspace{2em}} = 18$

$19 - 10 = \underline{\hspace{2em}}$ $10 + \underline{\hspace{2em}} = 20$ $19 - 9 = \underline{\hspace{2em}}$

$17 - 9 = \underline{\hspace{2em}}$ $18 - 9 = \underline{\hspace{2em}}$ $18 - 10 = \underline{\hspace{2em}}$

Partner Game—Number Quest

Getting Ready: Make two copies of the subtraction cards below and one copy of the game board on page 143 on colorful card stock. Cut out the game pieces along the dashed lines. Provide 10–12 identical game markers for each player.

Playing the Game: To begin the game, place the game board in the center of the playing area. Shuffle the subtraction facts cards and place them facedown in a pile on the game board. Give each player a set of game markers. To begin the game, Player A draws a card from the pile and then figures out the difference. For example, if the math fact is 15 – 10, the answer is 5. If the answer is correct, Player A covers the number 5 in one of the boxes. If the answer is already covered, Player A's turn is over. Player B should listen carefully to catch any errors. Player B then continues the game in the same manner. As a fun twist to the game, whenever a difference is 7, 8, or 9, the player covers two numbers that equal that number. The first player to cover three adjacent boxes in a horizontal, vertical, or diagonal row is declared the winner.

Make two copies.

16 – 10	13 – 10	19 – 10	16 – 9	13 – 9	
17 – 10	14 – 10	11 – 10	17 – 9	14 – 9	11 – 9
18 – 10	15 – 10	12 – 10	18 – 9	15 – 9	12 – 9

Number Quest

= ?

Cover three spaces in a ↑, →, ↗, or ↘ row to win. Note: For 7, 8, or 9, cover two numbers that equal that number.

3	5	6	3	6	4	2	1	2
4	1	4	2	5	2	3	6	3
5	6	2	5	1	3	4	5	4

Name ____________________ Date ____________________

Think and Solve

Thinking Strategies: How Far Apart? Count Back and Think Addition and Make 10—How Much More Is Needed?

0 1 2 3 4 5 6 7 8 9 10 11 12 13 14 15 16 17 18 19 20

Fold on line.

Directions

- Hide the number line by folding over the top of this paper.
- Work with a partner.
- Read each problem. Then, tell your partner how you will solve it.
- Write the answer in the blank.
- Use the number line to check your answers.

17 − 7 = ___	12 − 10 = ___	19 − 9 = ___	14 − 4 = ___	11 − 10 = ___
13 − 3 = ___	16 − 10 = ___	18 − 10 = ___	16 − 6 = ___	12 − 2 = ___
18 − 8 = ___	11 − 1 = ___	13 − 10 = ___	15 − 5 = ___	19 − 10 = ___

Name ______________________ Date ______________

Fast Facts 65

Minuends 11 to 20

The activity coordinates with page 144 and includes previously learned facts.

15 − 10 = ___ 14 − 4 = ___

19 − 9 = ___ 17 − 10 = ___

20 − 10 = ___ 14 − 10 = ___

15 − 5 = ___ 11 − 10 = ___ 12 − 2 = ___

13 − 10 = ___ 18 − 8 = ___ 19 − 10 = ___

Name ______________________ Date ______________

Fast Facts 66

Minuends 11 to 20

The activity coordinates with page 144 and includes previously learned facts.

11 − 1 = ___ 19 − 9 = ___

18 − 10 = ___ 16 − 10 = ___

16 − 6 = ___ 13 − 10 = ___

14 − 10 = ___ 12 − 10 = ___ 14 − 4 = ___

17 − 7 = ___ 17 − 10 = ___ 18 − 8 = ___

Think and Solve

Thinking Strategies: How Far Apart? Count Back and Think Addition and Make 10—How Much More Is Needed?

0 1 2 3 4 5 6 7 8 9 10 11 12 13 14 15 16 17 18 19 20

Fold on line.

Directions

- Hide the number line by folding over the top of this paper.
- Work with a partner.
- Read each problem. Then, tell your partner how you will solve it.
- Write the answer in the blank.
- Use the number line to check your answers.

16 − 7 = ___ 14 − 5 = ___ 12 − 9 = ___ 13 − 4 = ___

18 − 9 = ___ 15 − 9 = ___ 15 − 6 = ___ 16 − 9 = ___

17 − 9 = ___ 11 − 2 = ___ 14 − 9 = ___ 17 − 8 = ___

Name ______________________ Date ______________

Fast Facts 67

Minuends 11 to 20

The activity coordinates with page 146 and includes previously learned facts.

13 − 4 = ___ 16 − 9 = ___

17 − 8 = ___ 15 − 9 = ___

11 − 9 = ___ 12 − 3 = ___

14 − 5 = ___ 17 − 9 = ___ 11 − 2 = ___

12 − 9 = ___ 13 − 9 = ___ 16 − 7 = ___

Name ______________________ Date ______________

Fast Facts 68

Minuends 11 to 20

The activity coordinates with page 146 and includes previously learned facts.

17 − 8 = ___ 12 − 3 = ___

14 − 9 = ___ 17 − 9 = ___

16 − 9 = ___ 12 − 9 = ___

16 − 7 = ___ 13 − 4 = ___ 15 − 6 = ___

14 − 5 = ___ 11 − 2 = ___ 13 − 9 = ___

Name ______________________ Date ______________

Quick Check A

Minuends 11 to 20

The test is on facts from pages 136–147 and previously learned facts. Alternate it with Quick Check B.

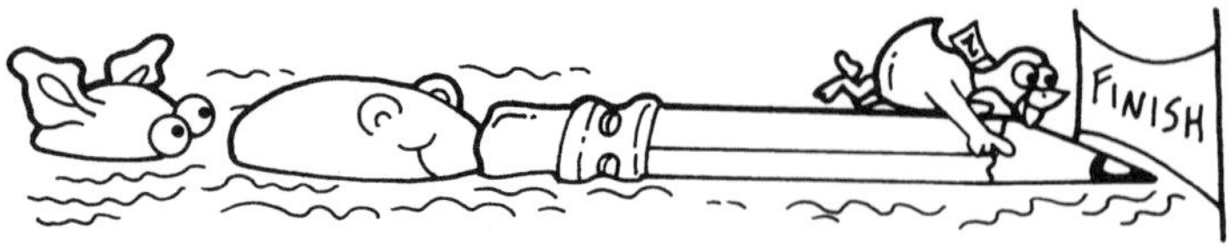

Score: __________

Time:

A	18 − 9	8 − 5	12 − 10	11 − 1	16 − 7	15 − 5
B	9 − 3	12 − 9	14 − 9	17 − 10	11 − 2	15 − 6
C	16 − 6	12 − 2	16 − 9	13 − 4	10 − 10	15 − 10
D	18 − 10	13 − 3	11 − 9	17 − 9	12 − 3	10 − 7
E	10 − 6	17 − 8	14 − 4	15 − 9	8 − 6	16 − 10
F	13 − 9	17 − 7	10 − 2	14 − 10	14 − 5	9 − 7

Name ______________________________ Date ________________

Quick Check B

Minuends 11 to 20

The test is on facts from pages 136–147 and previously learned facts. Alternate it with Quick Check A.

Score: __________

Time:

A	12 − 2	13 − 10	16 − 7	9 − 4	14 − 9	7 − 3
B	12 − 9	8 − 3	18 − 8	11 − 9	16 − 10	11 − 2
C	13 − 4	17 − 9	19 − 10	13 − 3	8 − 2	15 − 6
D	18 − 9	7 − 6	12 − 3	18 − 10	8 − 4	16 − 6
E	17 − 8	15 − 5	9 − 9	19 − 9	14 − 10	11 − 2
F	16 − 9	11 − 10	9 − 2	14 − 5	17 − 7	13 − 9

Think and Solve

Thinking Strategies: Think Addition and Use Double Facts and Make 10—How Much More Is Needed?

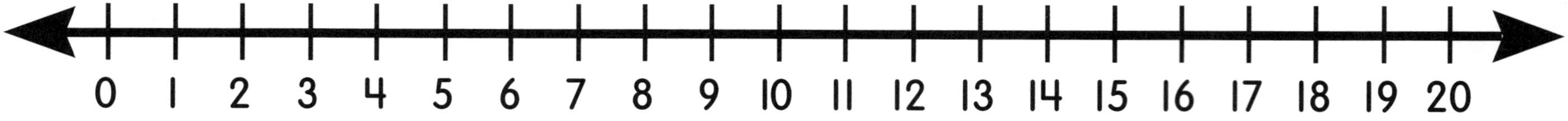

Fold on line.

Directions

- Hide the number line by folding over the top of this paper.
- Work with a partner.
- Read each problem. Then, tell your partner how you will solve it.
- Write the answer in the blank.
- Use the number line to check your answers.

$12 - 6 = \_\_\_\_$	$6 + \_\_\_\_ = 12$	$12 - 5 = \_\_\_\_$	$5 + \_\_\_\_ = 12$	$16 - 9 = \_\_\_\_$
$18 - 9 = \_\_\_\_$	$9 + \_\_\_\_ = 18$	$18 - 8 = \_\_\_\_$	$8 + \_\_\_\_ = 18$	$16 - 8 = \_\_\_\_$
$14 - 7 = \_\_\_\_$	$7 + \_\_\_\_ = 14$	$14 - 8 = \_\_\_\_$	$8 + \_\_\_\_ = 14$	$14 - 6 = \_\_\_\_$

Name ____________________ Date ____________

Fast Facts 69

Minuends 11 to 20

The activity coordinates with page 150 and includes previously learned facts.

12 − 6 = ___ 16 − 8 = ___

14 − 6 = ___ 14 − 8 = ___

16 − 9 = ___ 16 − 7 = ___

12 − 7 = ___ 18 − 8 = ___ 12 − 5 = ___

18 − 10 = ___ 14 − 7 = ___ 18 − 9 = ___

Name ____________________ Date ____________

Fast Facts 70

Minuends 11 to 20

The activity coordinates with page 150 and includes previously learned facts.

14 − 8 = ___ 18 − 10 = ___

18 − 9 = ___ 12 − 7 = ___

14 − 7 = ___ 16 − 9 = ___

16 − 8 = ___ 12 − 5 = ___ 18 − 8 = ___

12 − 6 = ___ 16 − 7 = ___ 14 − 6 = ___

Partner Game—On Target

Getting Ready: Copy the subtraction game cards below and the small game boards on page 153 onto colorful card stock. Cut out the game pieces along the dashed lines. Place the subtraction cards in a small paper bag.

Playing the Game: To begin the game, give each player three dartboards. Player A draws a card from the paper bag, answers the fact, and looks for the number on one of the dartboards. If a match is made, the game card is placed below the dartboard. If not, the game card is returned to the paper bag. Player B then takes a turn and continues the game in the same manner. The first player to hit one of the "targets" with three darts or hits three targets each with one dart is the winner.

Make one copy.

16 − 7	14 − 5	18 − 9	16 − 6	18 − 8	14 − 4
12 − 5	14 − 7	16 − 9	14 − 6	16 − 8	18 − 10
12 − 7	14 − 9	15 − 10	12 − 6	14 − 8	16 − 10

On Target
7

On Target
10

On Target
6

On Target
9

On Target
5

On Target
8

Name ______________________ Date ______________________

Quick Check C

Minuends 11 to 20

The test is on facts from page 150 and previously learned facts.
Alternate it with Quick Check D.

Score: ________

Time:

A	12 − 6	16 − 9	10 − 5	19 − 9	17 − 8	14 − 4
B	16 − 7	12 − 3	18 − 8	15 − 9	11 − 2	10 − 4
C	14 − 10	17 − 9	15 − 5	14 − 8	11 − 1	18 − 9
D	15 − 6	12 − 7	17 − 7	10 − 3	14 − 7	11 − 10
E	16 − 6	14 − 6	11 − 9	12 − 5	13 − 4	12 − 9
F	18 − 10	12 − 2	16 − 8	10 − 8	14 − 5	19 − 10

Name ______________________ Date ______________

Quick Check D Minuends 11 to 20

The test is on facts from page 150 and previously learned facts. Alternate it with Quick Check C.

Score: ______

Time:

A	14 − 4	11 − 9	14 − 7	20 − 10	18 − 9	9 − 5
B	18 − 10	12 − 7	13 − 9	17 − 8	16 − 6	9 − 6
C	16 − 8	13 − 4	16 − 10	12 − 3	18 − 8	15 − 9
D	17 − 9	14 − 8	10 − 6	13 − 3	15 − 6	12 − 5
E	12 − 6	17 − 10	14 − 9	11 − 1	16 − 7	12 − 9
F	15 − 5	16 − 9	10 − 7	14 − 6	19 − 9	13 − 10

Think and Solve

Thinking Strategy: Think Addition and Make 10—How Much More Is Needed?

0 1 2 3 4 5 6 7 8 9 10 11 12 13 14 15 16 17 18 19 20

Fold on line.

Directions

- Hide the number line by folding over the top of this paper.
- Work with a partner.
- Read each problem. Then, tell your partner how you will solve it.
- Write the answer in the blank.
- Use the number line to check your answers.

11 − 8 = ___ 8 + ___ = 11 14 − 8 = ___ 8 + ___ = 14

15 − 8 = ___ 8 + ___ = 15 17 − 8 = ___ 8 + ___ = 17

12 − 8 = ___ 8 + ___ = 12 13 − 8 = ___ 8 + ___ = 13

Name ______________________________ Date ______________

Fast Facts 71

Minuends 11 to 20

The activity coordinates with page 156.

14 − 8 = ___ 17 − 8 = ___

___ + 8 = 12 8 + ___ = 11

11 − 8 = ___ 13 − 8 = ___

___ + 8 = 15 8 + ___ = 14 8 + ___ = 17

8 + ___ = 13 12 − 8 = ___ 15 − 8 = ___

Name ______________________________ Date ______________

Fast Facts 72

Minuends 11 to 20

The activity coordinates with page 156.

___ + 8 = 17 8 + ___ = 15

15 − 8 = ___ 11 − 8 = ___

___ + 8 = 14 8 + ___ = 12

17 − 8 = ___ 13 − 8 = ___ 14 − 8 = ___

12 − 8 = ___ ___ + 8 = 11 ___ + 8 = 13

Name ____________________ Date ____________

Think and Solve

Thinking Strategy: Think Addition and Make 10—How Much More Is Needed?

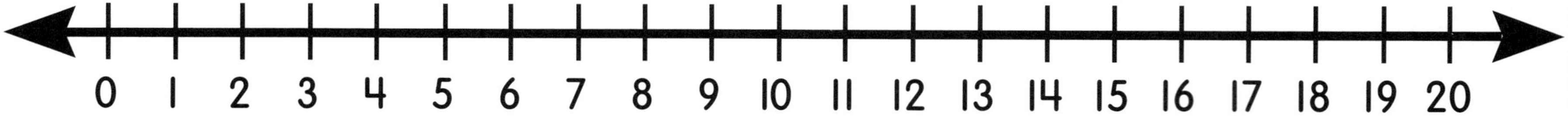

Fold on line.

Directions

- Hide the number line by folding over the top of this paper.
- Work with a partner.
- Read each problem. Then, tell your partner how you will solve it.
- Write the answer in the blank.
- Use the number line to check your answers.

11 – 7 = ____ 7 + ____ = 11 14 – 7 = ____ 7 + ____ = 14

16 – 7 = ____ 7 + ____ = 16 12 – 7 = ____ 7 + ____ = 12

13 – 7 = ____ 7 + ____ = 13 15 – 7 = ____ 7 + ____ = 15

Name ______________________ Date ______________

Fast Facts 73

Minuends 11 to 20

The activity coordinates with page 158 and includes previously learned facts.

11 − 7 = ___   7 + ___ = 12

___ + 7 = 14   16 − 7 = ___

15 − 7 = ___   14 − 7 = ___

___ + 7 = 16   7 + ___ = 11   13 − 7 = ___

7 + ___ = 15   12 − 7 = ___   7 + ___ = 13

Name ______________________ Date ______________

Fast Facts 74

Minuends 11 to 20

The activity coordinates with page 158 and includes previously learned facts.

___ + 7 = 13   14 − 7 = ___

12 − 7 = ___   7 + ___ = 16

___ + 7 = 15   13 − 7 = ___

16 − 7 = ___   11 − 7 = ___   ___ + 7 = 12

___ + 7 = 11   15 − 7 = ___   7 + ___ = 14

LAUNCH IT!

PLAYER A	PLAYER B
9	9
8	8
7	7
6	6
5	5
4	4
3	3

Partner Game—Launch It!

Getting Ready: Make one copy of the above game board and the dice on page 161 on colorful card stock. Cut out the game pieces along the dashed lines. To form each die, fold along the solid lines to make the edges of the cube and then glue the tabs under the numerals. Provide a set of seven game markers for each player.

Playing the Game: Give each player a set of game markers. Player A rolls the dice, makes a subtraction sentence with the numbers shown, verbalizes the math fact, and then covers the correct answer in a box. Player B should listen carefully to catch errors. If the number is already covered or if the answer is incorrect, Player A's turn is over. Player B then takes a turn and continues the game in the same manner. If the designated answer is already covered on the game board, the player cannot roll the dice again and therefore loses a turn. The first player to cover the seven boxes in a column "launches" the balloon and is declared the winner.

Minuend Die

Glue here.

15

11 | 12 | 13 | 14 | Glue here.

Glue here.

16

Subtrahend Die

Glue here.

Grounded! Lose a turn.

–7 | –8 | –7 | –8 | Glue here.

Glue here.

Choose any answer. Cover it.

Name ____________________ Date ____________________

Quick Check E

Minuends 11 to 20

The test is on facts from pages 156–159 and previously learned facts.
Alternate it with Quick Check F.

Score: ____________

Time:

A	18 − 9	11 − 8	15 − 9	11 − 1	14 − 7	12 − 2
B	13 − 7	12 − 10	14 − 9	15 − 8	12 − 6	16 − 7
C	12 − 3	11 − 7	17 − 7	12 − 5	16 − 9	14 − 8
D	12 − 8	17 − 9	16 − 10	15 − 7	14 − 5	16 − 8
E	11 − 9	17 − 8	15 − 6	13 − 9	16 − 6	12 − 7
F	14 − 6	13 − 4	11 − 2	13 − 8	19 − 9	12 − 9

Name ______________________ Date ______________

Quick Check F

Minuends 11 to 20

The test is on facts from pages 156–159 and previously learned facts. Alternate it with Quick Check E.

Score: ______

Time:

A	16 − 8	13 − 3	17 − 7	13 − 9	11 − 7	12 − 3
B	15 − 9	12 − 6	15 − 5	17 − 8	14 − 7	12 − 8
C	11 − 2	14 − 4	14 − 8	17 − 9	12 − 7	20 − 10
D	14 − 6	11 − 8	13 − 4	18 − 8	12 − 9	16 − 7
E	12 − 5	19 − 10	15 − 7	11 − 9	13 − 8	14 − 5
F	15 − 8	11 − 10	14 − 9	18 − 9	13 − 7	17 − 10

Name ____________________ Date ____________

Think and Solve

Thinking Strategies: How Far Apart? Count Back and Think Addition and Make 10—How Much More Is Needed?

0 1 2 3 4 5 6 7 8 9 10 11 12 13 14 15 16 17 18 19 20

Fold on line.

Directions

- Hide the number line by folding over the top of this paper.
- Work with a partner.
- Read each problem. Then, tell your partner how you will solve it.
- Write the answer in the blank.
- Use the number line to check your answers.

11 – 5 = ___	5 + ___ = 10	5 + ___ = 11	12 – 4 = ___	4 + ___ = 12
11 – 4 = ___	4 + ___ = 10	4 + ___ = 11	11 – 3 = ___	
13 – 6 = ___	6 + ___ = 10	6 + ___ = 13		
11 – 6 = ___	6 + ___ = 10	6 + ___ = 11		
13 – 5 = ___	5 + ___ = 10	5 + ___ = 13		

Name ______________________ Date ______________

Fast Facts 75

Minuends 11 to 20

The activity coordinates with page 164.

13 − 5 = ___ 12 − 4 = ___

11 − 4 = ___ 11 − 6 = ___

___ + 5 = 11 ___ + 6 = 13

13 − 6 = ___ 11 − 3 = ___ 4 + ___ = 11

3 + ___ = 11 ___ + 4 = 12 11 − 5 = ___

Name ______________________ Date ______________

Fast Facts 76

Minuends 11 to 20

The activity coordinates with page 164.

___ + 4 = 12 11 − 4 = ___

12 − 4 = ___ 13 − 6 = ___

11 − 3 = ___ 5 + ___ = 13

11 − 6 = ___ 6 + ___ = 13 ___ + 6 = 11

13 − 5 = ___ ___ + 4 = 11 11 − 5 = ___

Partner Game—Rev Up 'n' Race 7

Getting Ready: Make two copies of the subtraction game cards below and enlarge one copy of the game board on page 167 on colorful card stock. Cut out the game pieces along the dashed lines. Provide a "race car" game marker and seven small math counters for each player.

Playing the Game: Shuffle the cards and place them facedown in a pile. Give each player a race car game marker and seven math counters. Place the game board in the center of the playing area. To begin the game, Player A draws a game card and states the difference for the subtraction sentence. Player B should listen carefully to catch errors. If the answer is correct, Player A uses that answer and moves the game marker the corresponding number of spaces around the race track. If the answer is incorrect, Player A's turn is over. Player B then takes a turn and continues the game in the same manner. Whenever a player has circled the track in one complete lap, that player uses a counter to cover a number on the lap chart. The winner is the first player to complete seven laps.

Make two copies.

11 − 4	11 − 5	11 − 6	12 − 4	13 − 5	13 − 6
11 − 8	12 − 8	13 − 8	14 − 8	15 − 8	17 − 8
11 − 7	12 − 7	13 − 7	14 − 7	15 − 7	16 − 7

Player A Laps	1	2	3	4	5	6	7
Player B Laps	1	2	3	4	5	6	7

Name ______________________ Date ______________

Quick Check G

Minuends 11 to 20

The test is on facts from page 164 and previously learned facts. Alternate it with Quick Check H. The new facts are repeated for extra practice.

Score: ____________

Time:

A	11 − 5	14 − 9	12 − 4	14 − 5	13 − 7	13 − 5
B	15 − 8	11 − 3	12 − 5	13 − 6	11 − 6	14 − 8
C	12 − 7	11 − 4	12 − 8	14 − 7	12 − 4	11 − 2
D	11 − 8	13 − 6	15 − 7	12 − 3	15 − 9	11 − 5
E	13 − 5	17 − 8	14 − 6	11 − 4	17 − 9	12 − 6
F	11 − 7	13 − 8	11 − 6	13 − 4	15 − 10	11 − 3

Name ______________________________ Date ________________

Quick Check H

Minuends 11 to 20

The test is on facts from page 164 and previously learned facts. Alternate it with Quick Check G. The new facts are repeated for extra practice.

Time:

Score: __________

A	14 − 5	11 − 3	13 − 3	11 − 6	13 − 9	17 − 7
B	18 − 9	15 − 7	13 − 6	18 − 10	12 − 4	11 − 1
C	11 − 5	12 − 9	15 − 8	15 − 6	13 − 5	11 − 4
D	13 − 8	16 − 9	11 − 5	12 − 8	13 − 6	11 − 7
E	11 − 3	16 − 7	15 − 10	11 − 4	14 − 8	13 − 10
F	12 − 4	11 − 9	13 − 7	12 − 3	18 − 8	13 − 5

Name ______________________ Date ______________

50 Nifty Facts A

Minuends 11 to 20

Alternate this test with page 171.

A	11 − 3	13 − 6	16 − 8	14 − 4	12 − 9
B	14 − 9	11 − 1	12 − 7	17 − 8	11 − 6
C	17 − 7	15 − 8	11 − 2	12 − 4	14 − 10
D	13 − 5	11 − 8	12 − 10	15 − 9	13 − 7
E	16 − 10	14 − 5	18 − 8	15 − 7	17 − 9
F	13 − 3	11 − 7	16 − 9	13 − 4	12 − 5
G	12 − 8	14 − 6	11 − 9	15 − 10	16 − 7
H	18 − 10	16 − 6	18 − 9	14 − 8	11 − 5
I	15 − 6	13 − 10	14 − 7	12 − 6	15 − 5
J	13 − 8	12 − 3	20 − 10	13 − 9	11 − 4

Name ______________________ Date ______________

50 Nifty Facts B

Minuends 11 to 20

Alternate this test with page 170.

A	18 − 9	12 − 2	15 − 10	11 − 2	14 − 7
B	13 − 3	15 − 9	12 − 5	11 − 10	12 − 4
C	20 − 10	11 − 4	16 − 7	17 − 9	12 − 6
D	12 − 9	13 − 7	14 − 4	11 − 5	15 − 6
E	13 − 8	17 − 10	14 − 5	16 − 8	13 − 6
F	14 − 10	17 − 8	11 − 9	18 − 8	15 − 7
G	11 − 3	16 − 6	14 − 9	12 − 8	13 − 5
H	13 − 4	11 − 7	13 − 10	14 − 6	16 − 9
I	14 − 8	17 − 7	13 − 9	11 − 8	12 − 3
J	11 − 6	15 − 8	12 − 7	15 − 5	19 − 10

Answer Key

Page 7
A. 9, 2, 8, 10, 10, 6, 4
B. 8, 8, 7, 10, 8, 5, 5
C. 10, 3, 8, 8, 6, 7, 10
D. 9, 9, 9, 6, 9, 10, 5
E. 3, 7, 6, 9, 8, 9, 6
F. 4, 10, 10, 5, 8, 4, 10
G. 9, 7, 7, 8, 7, 4, 5

Page 9
Row 1: 1, 8, 3, 9, 6
Row 2: 8, 4, 6, 2, 5

Page 10
Row 1: 5, 9, 2, 6, 9
Row 2: 7, 7, 10, 10, 8

Page 11
Fast Facts 1
Row 1: 3, 6
Row 2: 7, 5
Row 3: 5, 4
Row 4: 9, 10, 5
Row 5: 6, 7, 8
Fast Facts 2
Row 1: 7, 3
Row 2: 6, 4
Row 3: 10, 8
Row 4: 4, 4, 9
Row 5: 9, 10, 8

Page 12
Row 1: 5, 10, 6, 4, 9
Row 2: 7, 8, 2, 10, 9

Page 13
Fast Facts 3
Row 1: 8, 4
Row 2: 7, 5
Row 3: 10, 5
Row 4: 10, 6, 9
Row 5: 3, 8, 6
Fast Facts 4
Row 1: 4, 3
Row 2: 7, 9
Row 3: 10, 7
Row 4: 4, 6, 8
Row 5: 9, 5, 5

Page 14
Row 1: 5, 9, 6, 6, 9
Row 2: 8, 9, 7, 6, 8
Row 3: 8, 9, 7, 5, 8
Row 4: 5, 10, 10, 7, 9

Page 15
Fast Facts 5
Row 1: 9, 6
Row 2: 5, 10
Row 3: 3, 7
Row 4: 6, 2, 5
Row 5: 4, 5, 7
Fast Facts 6
Row 1: 10, 8
Row 2: 5, 4
Row 3: 4, 8
Row 4: 8, 7, 6
Row 5: 7, 10, 5

Page 18
A. 10, 6, 6, 9, 3, 10
B. 10, 8, 7, 2, 6, 7
C. 4, 5, 8, 8, 3, 8
D. 9, 5, 9, 7, 5, 7
E. 1, 6, 6, 9, 3, 10
F. 5, 4, 9, 10, 7, 8

Page 19
A. 8, 10, 4, 6, 5, 8
B. 10, 10, 8, 6, 9, 8
C. 5, 4, 6, 9, 10, 5
D. 9, 3, 6, 7, 5, 3
E. 7, 4, 9, 3, 7, 9
F. 2, 9, 10, 7, 4, 7

Page 20
Row 1: 10, 4, 9, 1, 2
Row 2: 3, 6, 5, 8, 7

Page 21
Row 1: 8, 2, 7, 3, 0
Row 2: 9, 6, 4, 1, 5

Page 22
Fast Facts 7
Row 1: 10, 7
Row 2: 3, 5
Row 3: 9, 8
Row 4: 7, 5, 4
Row 5: 2, 9, 6
Fast Facts 8
Row 1: 7, 10
Row 2: 3, 5
Row 3: 7, 8
Row 4: 3, 9, 0
Row 5: 6, 5, 9

Page 25
A. 6, 5, 10, 3, 9, 10
B. 8, 9, 9, 7, 2, 6
C. 6, 9, 4, 8, 5, 7
D. 0, 10, 7, 10, 8, 7
E. 7, 6, 8, 9, 9, 3
F. 4, 9, 8, 6, 7, 10

Page 26
A. 8, 9, 10, 5, 7, 7
B. 9, 6, 10, 9, 7, 2
C. 1, 6, 10, 4, 6, 8
D. 10, 10, 5, 8, 7, 5
E. 7, 8, 9, 9, 6, 3
F. 7, 9, 6, 6, 3, 9

Page 27
Row 1: 8, 10, 9, 9, 8
Row 2: 9, 6, 7, 9, 8

Page 28
Fast Facts 9
Row 1: 8, 7
Row 2: 5, 9
Row 3: 8, 7
Row 4: 9, 9, 8
Row 5: 6, 10, 9
Fast Facts 10
Row 1: 9, 9;
Row 2: 7, 5
Row 3: 10, 8;
Row 4: 7, 8, 8
Row 5: 6, 9, 9

Page 29
Row 1: 10, 9, 10, 8, 10
Row 2: 10, 8, 10, 8, 9

Page 30
Fast Facts 11
Row 1: 10, 10
Row 2: 6, 7
Row 3: 9, 10
Row 4: 10, 10, 10
Row 5: 8, 9, 8
Fast Facts 12
Row 1: 10, 10
Row 2: 9, 6
Row 3: 8, 10
Row 4: 10, 7, 8
Row 5: 10, 9, 10

Page 33
A. 10, 9, 10, 9, 6, 8
B. 7, 10, 8, 10, 5, 8
C. 8, 10, 5, 9, 10, 7
D. 5, 6, 10, 9, 8, 10
E. 9, 5, 10, 4, 9, 10
F. 8, 7, 10, 8, 4, 9

Page 34
A. 7, 10, 7, 10, 8, 9
B. 8, 8, 10, 6, 10, 9
C. 9, 10, 8, 10, 7, 8
D. 7, 9, 10, 8, 5, 10
E. 9, 10, 7, 8, 10, 4
F. 9, 5, 10, 7, 9, 8

Page 35
A. 9, 10, 9, 5, 8
B. 7, 7, 10, 6, 10
C. 7, 8, 6, 9, 9
D. 4, 6, 10, 9, 5
E. 8, 10, 7, 5, 7
F. 6, 7, 8, 6, 9
G. 8, 6, 1, 7, 9
H. 5, 10, 10, 3, 10
I. 4, 8, 10, 8, 10
J. 8, 6, 10, 4, 9

Page 36
A. 8, 9, 6, 8, 10
B. 8, 9, 7, 10, 6
C. 10, 7, 5, 9, 5
D. 7, 8, 10, 9, 6
E. 8, 10, 4, 9, 5
F. 10, 8, 6, 4, 9
G. 7, 3, 7, 10, 6
H. 5, 8, 9, 10, 7
I. 10, 7, 9, 4, 8
J. 2, 0, 9, 4, 2

Page 37
Row 1: 0, 1, 0, 1, 0
Row 2: 1, 1, 0, 1, 0
Row 3: 0, 1, 1, 1, 0

Page 38
Fast Facts 13
Row 1: 6, 1
Row 2: 1, 1
Row 3: 0, 0
Row 4: 1, 1, 0
Row 5: 1, 0, 1
Fast Facts 14
Row 1: 0, 0
Row 2: 1, 1,
Row 3: 1, 0
Row 4: 1, 1, 1
Row 5: 0, 0, 0

Page 39
Row 1: 2, 1, 1, 2, 2
Row 2: 0, 1, 2, 1, 0
Row 3: 2, 0, 2, 2, 0

Page 40
Fast Facts 15
Row 1: 2, 0
Row 2: 2, 2
Row 3: 2, 1
Row 4: 0, 2, 2
Row 5: 1, 2, 0
Fast Facts 16
Row 1: 2, 0
Row 2: 2, 2
Row 3: 1, 1
Row 4: 2, 2, 2
Row 5: 1, 2, 0

Page 41
Row 1: 3, 3, 1, 2, 2
Row 2: 2, 2, 3, 2, 3
Row 3: 5, 1, 2, 3, 3

Page 42
Fast Facts 17
Row 1: 2, 2
Row 2: 3, 0
Row 3: 3, 1
Row 4: 4, 3, 3
Row 5: 3, 8, 3
Fast Facts 18
Row 1: 1, 3
Row 2: 3, 3
Row 3: 2, 1
Row 4: 2, 2, 3
Row 5: 3, 1, 3

Page 43
Row 1: 1, 3
Row 2: 2, 3
Row 3: 0, 1, 2
Row 4: 2, 3, 1
Row 5: 10, 5, 10
Row 6: 7, 7, 9
Row 7: 7, 8, 6
Row 8: 8, 9, 9
Row 9: 3, 2, 2
Row 10: 3, 2, 3
Row 11: 3, 1, 2
Row 12: 2, 3, 1

Page 44
Row 1: 5, 6, 3, 8, 3
Row 2: 1, 7, 0, 0, 5
Row 3: 6, 4, 2, 10, 9

Page 45
Fast Facts 19
Row 1: 5, 3
Row 2: 4, 2
Row 3: 7, 6
Row 4: 6, 7, 1
Row 5: 1, 8, 10
Fast Facts 20
Row 1: 8, 6
Row 2: 3, 3
Row 3: 2, 9
Row 4: 5, 6, 0
Row 5: 1, 4, 7

Answer Key

Page 46
Row 1: 2, 2, 1, 4, 2
Row 2: 4, 5, 1, 3, 4
Row 3: 3, 5, 3, 3, 5

Page 47
Fast Facts 21
Row 1: 4, 4
Row 2: 5, 2
Row 3: 4, 3
Row 4: 3, 3, 4
Row 5: 5, 5, 3
Fast Facts 22
Row 1: 3, 3
Row 2: 2, 4
Row 3: 5, 2
Row 4: 3, 1, 4
Row 5: 5, 3, 5

Page 50
Row 1: 2, 3
Row 2: 5, 5
Row 3: 4, 3, 1
Row 4: 4, 5, 7
Row 5: 8, 10, 8
Row 6: 10, 7, 10
Row 7: 9, 3, 6
Row 8: 9, 10, 10
Row 9: 8, 2, 6
Row 10: 1, 4, 3
Row 11: 3, 3, 9
Row 12: 0, 1, 6

Page 52
A. 3, 1, 7, 4, 6, 2, 6
B. 4, 1, 5, 3, 3, 7, 3
C. 6, 7, 4, 1, 0, 7, 4
D. 2, 3, 0, 8, 5, 1, 2
E. 4, 5, 3, 6, 2, 3, 8
F. 2, 9, 5, 4, 2, 5, 1
G. 1, 0, 2, 6, 9, 1, 1

Page 54
Row 1: 1, 8, 1, 5, 9
Row 2: 6, 2, 6, 2, 3
Row 3: 4, 7, 7, 5, 8

Page 55
Row 1: 4, 0, 3, 8, 1
Row 2: 7, 5, 5, 6, 8
Row 3: 0, 9, 7, 4, 6

Page 56
Fast Facts 23
Row 1: 9, 4
Row 2: 7, 2
Row 3: 3, 7
Row 4: 4, 9, 0
Row 5: 6, 5, 6
Fast Facts 24
Row 1: 1, 2
Row 2: 3, 8
Row 3: 8, 5
Row 4: 5, 8, 10
Row 5: 1, 7, 6

Page 59
Row 1: 0, 7, 5, 3, 7
Row 2: 5, 3, 8, 4, 1
Row 3: 6, 2, 1, 6, 4

Page 60
Fast Facts 25
Row 1: 6, 6
Row 2: 0, 2
Row 3: 4, 5
Row 4: 0, 8, 1
Row 5: 1, 4, 7
Fast Facts 26
Row 1: 0, 4
Row 2: 3, 1
Row 3: 5, 6
Row 4: 2, 2, 3
Row 5: 5, 7, 7

Page 61
A. 1, 9, 2, 5, 5, 3
B. 5, 3, 6, 2, 0, 3
C. 7, 2, 8, 4, 8, 1
D. 7, 9, 5, 1, 2, 8
E. 1, 6, 0, 6, 7, 4
F. 7, 4, 6, 0, 10, 4

Page 62
A. 0, 6, 4, 0, 8, 1
B. 3, 8, 0, 0, 5, 6
C. 7, 1, 7, 6, 2, 5
D. 3, 3, 10, 5, 2, 9
E. 7, 4, 2, 5, 2, 4
F. 1, 3, 7, 8, 1, 4

Page 63
Row 1: 1, 0, 1, 8, 1
Row 2: 4, 0, 1, 1, 1
Row 3: 7, 1, 0, 1, 0

Page 64
Fast Facts 27
Row 1: 0, 0
Row 2: 5, 1
Row 3: 1, 5
Row 4: 7, 1, 0
Row 5: 10, 1, 1
Fast Facts 28
Row 1: 1, 9
Row 2: 0, 1
Row 3: 1, 1
Row 4: 6, 3, 0
Row 5: 0, 1, 0

Page 65
Row 1: 2, 8, 1, 2, 2
Row 2: 2, 5, 2, 1, 1
Row 3: 7, 2, 4, 2, 2

Page 66
Fast Facts 29
Row 1: 4, 2
Row 2: 2, 8
Row 3: 2, 2
Row 4: 1, 2, 1
Row 5: 6, 1, 2
Fast Facts 30
Row 1: 1, 2
Row 2: 2, 7
Row 3: 3, 1
Row 4: 3, 2, 2
Row 5: 2, 5, 2

Page 69
A. 2, 6, 1, 6, 2, 0
B. 4, 2, 0, 7, 2, 1
C. 6, 7, 2, 1, 0, 2
D. 0, 2, 1, 1, 4, 10
E. 0, 4, 5, 2, 1, 1
F. 1, 3, 3, 0, 2, 0

Page 70
A. 2, 1, 7, 8, 0, 1
B. 0, 2, 4, 2, 0, 5
C. 7, 1, 0, 8, 1, 2
D. 1, 8, 2, 1, 0, 1
E. 0, 2, 6, 7, 1, 3
F. 2, 4, 0, 6, 1, 9

Page 71
Row 1: 4, 5, 6
Row 2: 4, 3, 4, 2, 8
Row 3: 7, 3, 2, 2

Page 72
Fast Facts 31
Row 1: 5, 4
Row 2: 3, 4
Row 3: 8, 4
Row 4: 6, 2, 7
Row 5: 2, 2, 3
Fast Facts 32
Row 1: 2, 5
Row 2: 7, 2
Row 3: 3, 2
Row 4: 4, 6, 3
Row 5: 4, 4, 8

Page 73
A. 5, 6, 4, 3, 3, 2
B. 1, 0, 2, 2, 0, 7
C. 1, 4, 5, 4, 7, 1
D. 6, 6, 2, 4, 2, 1
E. 2, 7, 3, 1, 2, 3
F. 4, 2, 8, 8, 5, 3

Page 74
A. 4, 0, 5, 6, 7, 6
B. 2, 7, 4, 2, 5, 0
C. 9, 7, 3, 1, 0, 1
D. 3, 6, 0, 5, 4, 5
E. 3, 0, 3, 8, 2, 6
F. 4, 4, 1, 4, 7, 7

Page 75
Row 1: 9, 6, 9, 3, 5
Row 2: 4, 8, 5, 8, 3
Row 3: 9, 4, 9, 5
Row 4: 7, 4, 7, 3

Page 76
Fast Facts 33
Row 1: 6, 5
Row 2: 3, 3
Row 3: 5, 6
Row 4: 4, 5, 4
Row 5: 3, 4, 3
Fast Facts 34
Row 1: 6, 5
Row 2: 5, 5
Row 3: 3, 3
Row 4: 4, 3, 3
Row 5: 4, 4, 4

Page 77
Fast Facts 35
Row 1: 7, 4
Row 2: 5, 3
Row 3: 6, 3
Row 4: 4, 3, 6
Row 5: 4, 5, 5
Fast Facts 36
Row 1: 6, 3
Row 2: 3, 6
Row 3: 3, 5
Row 4: 3, 5, 4
Row 5: 5, 7, 4

Page 80
A. 5, 2, 4, 3, 5, 0
B. 3, 6, 1, 0, 3, 3
C. 4, 8, 5, 5, 4, 4
D. 6, 6, 4, 2, 2, 3
E. 5, 3, 3, 1, 4, 2
F. 3, 5, 1, 8, 5, 0

Page 81
A. 4, 3, 6, 5, 3, 4
B. 7, 4, 3, 1, 3, 6
C. 4, 2, 3, 3, 6, 5
D. 5, 1, 3, 4, 2, 5
E. 3, 6, 4, 8, 1, 0
F. 3, 0, 5, 5, 4, 9

Page 82
A. 5, 2, 4, 0, 3
B. 2, 4, 4, 2, 7
C. 2, 3, 4, 4, 2
D. 1, 8, 5, 2, 0
E. 2, 3, 7, 5, 5
F. 8, 1, 8, 3, 3
G. 7, 6, 1, 5, 5
H. 1, 2, 1, 1, 0
I. 6, 6, 3, 6, 1
J. 1, 3, 9, 4, 0

Page 83
A. 3, 0, 6, 1, 3
B. 1, 5, 6, 3, 6
C. 10, 5, 8, 0, 6
D. 4, 0, 1, 3, 3
E. 1, 2, 2, 1, 7
F. 4, 7, 4, 1, 0
G. 4, 0, 4, 0, 2
H. 2, 7, 0, 2, 5
I. 1, 7, 2, 9, 9
J. 5, 2, 4, 5, 0

Page 85
A. 11, 18, 11, 11, 12, 11, 15
B. 19, 15, 14, 11, 13, 11, 13
C. 13, 17, 12, 13, 12, 15, 17
D. 18, 13, 16, 13, 14, 12, 12
E. 12, 14, 12, 11, 16, 11, 17
F. 14, 16, 11, 16, 14, 14, 15
G. 11, 20, 14, 19, 15, 12, 13

Page 87
Row 1: 11, 10, 12, 11
Row 2: 13, 12, 11, 10
Row 3: 11, 12, 13, 12

Page 88
Fast Facts 37
Row 1: 12, 12
Row 2: 12, 13
Row 3: 11, 10
Row 4: 11, 12, 13
Row 5: 10, 11, 11
Fast Facts 38
Row 1: 11, 12
Row 2: 10, 11
Row 3: 12, 11
Row 4: 11, 12, 12
Row 5: 13, 10, 13

Page 89
Row 1: 14, 13, 16, 15
Row 2: 15, 14, 14, 13
Row 3: 15, 13, 14, 15

Page 90
Fast Facts 39
Row 1: 16, 15
Row 2: 13, 14
Row 3: 16, 14
Row 4: 15, 13, 14
Row 5: 15, 15, 14
Fast Facts 40
Row 1: 15, 14
Row 2: 16, 15
Row 3: 13, 16
Row 4: 13, 14, 14
Row 5: 15, 14, 15

Page 91
A. 14, 7, 12, 10, 11, 15
B. 11, 8, 13, 9, 13, 15
C. 14, 12, 9, 16, 7, 12
D. 14, 9, 11, 11, 8, 14
E. 10, 16, 10, 13, 12, 10
F. 15, 5, 15, 10, 6, 13

Answer Key

Page 92
A. 15, 13, 6, 15, 8, 15
B. 0, 9, 10, 7, 12, 12
C. 13, 15, 10, 13, 6, 10
D. 10, 11, 14, 11, 9, 14
E. 12, 11, 6, 13, 16, 9
F. 12, 10, 14, 8, 11, 14

Page 93
Row 1: 19, 18, 17, 16
Row 2: 18, 17, 19, 20
Row 3: 17, 16, 18, 17

Page 94
Fast Facts 41
Row 1: 20, 18
Row 2: 17, 16
Row 3: 18, 18
Row 4: 16, 17, 17
Row 5: 19, 19, 17
Fast Facts 42
Row 1: 17, 16
Row 2: 19, 20
Row 3: 18, 17
Row 4: 18, 16, 18
Row 5: 17, 17, 19

Page 97
A. 20, 10, 9, 17, 8, 19
B. 10, 18, 15, 13, 6, 16
C. 10, 18, 15, 9, 11, 17
D. 14, 6, 16, 11, 19, 5
E. 17, 10, 13, 17, 5, 12
F. 12, 18, 8, 16, 8, 14

Page 98
A. 18, 7, 17, 9, 12, 14
B. 11, 19, 9, 16, 6, 13
C. 17, 10, 17, 14, 7, 12
D. 13, 16, 11, 18, 9, 15
E. 11, 8, 19, 8, 15, 17
F. 20, 8, 10, 18, 9, 16

Page 99
Row 1: 10, 11, 12, 11, 13
Row 2: 14, 15, 13, 16, 17
Row 3: 15, 18, 19, 17

Page 100
Fast Facts 43
Row 1: 12, 15
Row 2: 13, 17
Row 3: 17, 14
Row 4: 11, 15, 13
Row 5: 19, 11, 18
Fast Facts 44
Row 1: 15, 11
Row 2: 11, 17
Row 3: 14, 13
Row 4: 16, 15, 18
Row 5: 12, 17, 13

Page 101
Fast Facts 45
Row 1: 18, 19
Row 2: 11, 13
Row 3: 13, 17
Row 4: 17, 15, 16
Row 5: 12, 11, 15
Fast Facts 46
Row 1: 15, 11
Row 2: 18, 15
Row 3: 14, 11
Row 4: 12, 17, 16
Row 5: 17, 13, 13

Page 104
A. 16, 16, 7, 16, 11, 9
B. 17, 11, 17, 9, 14, 15
C. 17, 18, 3, 11, 5, 17
D. 14, 15, 9, 20, 10, 10
E. 10, 8, 12, 18, 13, 15
F. 13, 12, 7, 9, 13, 19

Page 105
A. 14, 18, 10, 17, 4, 10
B. 15, 15, 10, 16, 8, 13
C. 9, 8, 19, 16, 7, 15
D. 13, 18, 5, 14, 5, 11
E. 17, 8, 20, 11, 13, 15
F. 11, 12, 10, 9, 12, 19

Page 106
Row 1: 10, 12, 14, 11, 13
Row 2: 13, 11, 10, 12, 14

Page 107
Fast Facts 47
Row 1: 10, 13
Row 2: 14, 11
Row 3: 12, 10
Row 4: 13, 10, 12
Row 5: 11, 11, 14
Fast Facts 48
Row 1: 10, 13
Row 2: 14, 11
Row 3: 11, 12
Row 4: 11, 12, 13
Row 5: 14, 10, 10

Page 108
A. 13, 12, 10, 14, 17, 6
B. 19, 14, 11, 10, 11, 15
C. 12, 14, 10, 12, 11, 17
D. 12, 14, 17, 12, 8, 15
E. 14, 13, 8, 11, 15, 18
F. 18, 13, 10, 13, 9, 16

Page 109
A. 15, 11, 9, 13, 11, 11
B. 15, 12, 17, 7, 10, 13
C. 13, 12, 12, 10, 16, 16
D. 10, 13, 18, 10, 13, 14
E. 17, 12, 9, 15, 19, 14
F. 14, 9, 11, 11, 14, 13

Page 110
Row 1: 10, 13, 10, 11, 12
Row 2: 11, 12, 14, 13, 15

Page 111
Fast Facts 49
Row 1: 11, 11
Row 2: 14, 13
Row 3: 15, 10
Row 4: 12, 12, 13
Row 5: 16, 15, 10
Fast Facts 50
Row 1: 13, 12
Row 2: 10, 11
Row 3: 11, 12
Row 4: 15, 14, 13
Row 5: 12, 15, 10

Page 114
A. 12, 18, 13, 12, 11, 15
B. 14, 11, 11, 17, 11, 13
C. 13, 12, 12, 16, 13, 13
D. 11, 14, 16, 11, 16, 11
E. 11, 12, 12, 12, 14, 15
F. 18, 13, 16, 14, 12, 15

Page 115
A. 11, 14, 14, 19, 12, 15
B. 13, 12, 16, 11, 17, 11
C. 17, 11, 11, 13, 16, 13
D. 15, 12, 11, 14, 12, 12
E. 11, 15, 11, 13, 20, 17
F. 11, 13, 12, 14, 12, 14

Page 116
A. 11, 18, 17, 11, 16
B. 13, 11, 14, 15, 12
C. 14, 11, 12, 17, 14
D. 13, 13, 11, 12, 12
E. 12, 15, 17, 13, 15
F. 16, 14, 13, 13, 11
G. 20, 15, 16, 12, 14
H. 11, 15, 11, 12, 19
I. 14, 13, 16, 14, 12
J. 13, 11, 18, 15, 17

Page 117
A. 12, 14, 12, 11, 17
B. 19, 11, 18, 13, 11
C. 14, 12, 12, 11, 13
D. 18, 12, 15, 20, 13
E. 12, 16, 12, 11, 15
F. 16, 14, 12, 11, 17
G. 11, 19, 15, 15, 13
H. 16, 11, 13, 16, 13
I. 16, 13, 17, 14, 11
J. 14, 12, 15, 14, 11

Page 118
A. 3, 0, 10
B. 8, 2, 9
C. 3, 3, 0
D. 0, 2, 10
E. 9, 3, 9

Page 119
Fast Facts 51
Row 1: 10, 2
Row 2: 8, 9
Row 3: 0, 3
Row 4: 9, 0, 17
Row 5: 3, 0, 9
Fast Facts 52
Row 1: 2, 0
Row 2: 9, 10
Row 3: 13, 8
Row 4: 3, 0, 10
Row 5: 1, 2, 9

Page 120
A. 5, 8, 10
B. 7, 4, 5
C. 5, 5, 4
D. 8, 4, 4
E. 4, 5, 4

Page 121
Fast Facts 53
Row 1: 10, 4
Row 2: 5, 8
Row 3: 4, 5
Row 4: 4, 5, 8
Row 5: 9, 4, 4
Fast Facts 54
Row 1: 7, 5
Row 2: 9, 5
Row 3: 7, 5
Row 4: 7, 9, 10
Row 5: 9, 8, 4

Page 122
Row 1: 2, 14
Row 2: 7, 9
Row 3: 10, 9, 4
Row 4: 3, 8, 4
Row 5: 11, 13, 17
Row 6: 14, 12, 15
Row 7: 11, 12, 11
Row 8: 12, 20, 14
Row 9: 9, 0, 8
Row 10: 1, 7, 10
Row 11: 4, 5, 3
Row 12: 3, 9, 5

Page 123
A. 10, 8, 6
B. 6, 8, 7
C. 8, 9, 7
D. 8, 6, 10
E. 9, 6, 10

Page 124
Fast Facts 55
Row 1: 9, 10
Row 2: 8, 7
Row 3: 6, 9
Row 4: 7, 8, 6
Row 5: 10, 7, 6
Fast Facts 56
Row 1: 10, 9
Row 2: 8, 7
Row 3: 7, 8
Row 4: 7, 10, 6
Row 5: 6, 6, 10

Page 125
A. 8, 10, 8
B. 6, 9, 6
C. 8, 7, 9
D. 9, 7, 10
E. 7, 6, 6

Page 126
Fast Facts 57
Row 1: 9, 9
Row 2: 7, 7
Row 3: 8, 6
Row 4: 8, 7, 6
Row 5: 8, 5, 9
Fast Facts 58
Row 1: 8, 6
Row 2: 7, 9
Row 3: 7, 6
Row 4: 5, 10, 8
Row 5: 7, 7, 10

Page 127
Row 1: 10, 6
Row 2: 10, 6
Row 3: 6, 7, 10
Row 4: 9, 7, 9
Row 5: 16, 18, 11
Row 6: 16, 13, 18
Row 7: 15, 20, 17
Row 8: 15, 17, 19
Row 9: 8, 9, 6
Row 10: 10, 7, 6
Row 11: 8, 8, 9
Row 12: 8, 9, 7

Page 134
A. 10, 9, 7, 5, 6, 3, 7
B. 9, 5, 4, 8, 10, 7, 2
C. 10, 9, 6, 4, 8, 4, 9
D. 8, 4, 9, 5, 6, 8, 10
E. 7, 7, 10, 6, 9, 3, 7
F. 3, 10, 9, 8, 8, 6, 8
G. 7, 10, 5, 8, 9, 2, 10

Page 136
Row 1: 1, 1, 2, 2
Row 2: 2, 2, 3, 3
Row 3: 3, 3, 4, 4

Page 137
Fast Facts 59
Row 1: 2, 2
Row 2: 2, 2
Row 3: 1, 3
Row 4: 3, 1, 3
Row 5: 4, 4, 3
Fast Facts 60
Row 1: 4, 2
Row 2: 2, 2
Row 3: 2, 3
Row 4: 4, 1, 3
Row 5: 1, 3, 3

Answer Key

Page 138
Row 1: 5, 5, 4, 4
Row 2: 7, 7, 6, 6
Row 3: 6, 6, 5, 5

Page 139
Fast Facts 61
Row 1: 7, 5
Row 2: 7, 5
Row 3: 5, 4
Row 4: 6, 4, 6
Row 5: 5, 6, 6
Fast Facts 62
Row 1: 6, 7
Row 2: 6, 5
Row 3: 6, 5
Row 4: 4, 4, 5
Row 5: 6, 7, 5

Page 140
Row 1: 10, 10, 8, 8
Row 2: 8, 8, 9, 9
Row 3: 7, 7
, 9, 9

Page 141
Fast Facts 63
Row 1: 7, 10
Row 2: 10, 9
Row 3: 10, 9
Row 4: 8, 8, 7
Row 5: 8, 8, 10
Fast Facts 64
Row 1: 9, 8
Row 2: 10, 7
Row 3: 9, 8
Row 4: 9, 10, 10
Row 5: 8, 9, 8

Page 144
Row 1: 10, 2, 10, 10, 1
Row 2: 10, 6, 8, 10, 10
Row 3: 10, 10, 3, 10, 9

Page 145
Fast Facts 65
Row 1: 5, 10
Row 2: 10, 7
Row 3: 10, 4
Row 4: 10, 1, 10
Row 5: 3, 10, 9
Fast Facts 66
Row 1: 10, 10
Row 2: 8, 6
Row 3: 10, 3
Row 4: 4, 2, 10
Row 5: 10, 7, 10

Page 146
Row 1: 9, 9, 3, 9
Row 2: 9, 6, 9, 7
Row 3: 8, 9, 5, 9

Page 147
Fast Facts 67
Row 1: 9, 7
Row 2: 9, 6
Row 3: 2, 9
Row 4: 9, 8, 9
Row 5: 3, 4, 9
Fast Facts 68
Row 1: 9, 9
Row 2: 5, 8
Row 3: 7, 3
Row 4: 9, 9, 9
Row 5: 9, 9, 4

Page 148
A. 9, 3, 2, 10, 9, 10
B. 6, 3, 5, 7, 9, 9
C. 10, 10, 7, 9, 0, 5
D. 8, 10, 2, 8, 9, 3
E. 4, 9, 10, 6, 2, 6
F. 4, 10, 8, 4, 9, 2

Page 149
A. 10, 3, 9, 5, 5, 4
B. 3, 5, 10, 2, 6, 9
C. 9, 8, 9, 10, 6, 9
D. 9, 1, 9, 8, 4, 10
E. 9, 10, 0, 10, 4, 9
F. 7, 1, 7, 9, 10, 4

Page 150
Row 1: 6, 6, 7, 7, 7
Row 2: 9, 9, 10, 10, 8
Row 3: 7, 7, 6, 6, 8

Page 151
Fast Facts 69
Row 1: 6, 8
Row 2: 8, 6
Row 3: 7, 9
Row 4: 5, 10, 7
Row 5: 8, 7, 9
Fast Facts 70
Row 1: 6, 8
Row 2: 9, 5
Row 3: 7, 7
Row 4: 8, 7, 10
Row 5: 6, 9, 8

Page 154
A. 6, 7, 5, 10, 9, 10
B. 9, 9, 10, 6, 9, 6
C. 4, 8, 10, 6, 10, 9
D. 9, 5, 10, 7, 7, 1
E. 10, 8, 2, 7, 9, 3
F. 8, 10, 8, 2, 9, 9

Page 155
A. 10, 2, 7, 10, 9, 4
B. 8, 5, 4, 9, 10, 3
C. 8, 9, 6, 9, 10, 6
D. 8, 6, 4, 10, 9, 7
E. 6, 7, 5, 10, 9, 3
F. 10, 7, 3, 8, 10, 3

Page 156
Row 1: 3, 3, 6, 6
Row 2: 7, 7, 9, 9
Row 3: 4, 4, 5, 5

Page 157
Fast Facts 71
Row 1: 6, 9
Row 2: 4, 3
Row 3: 3, 5
Row 4: 7, 6, 9
Row 5: 5, 4, 7
Fast Facts 72
Row 1: 9, 7
Row 2: 7, 3
Row 3: 6, 4
Row 4; 9, 5, 6
Row 5: 4, 3, 5

Page 158
Row 1: 4, 4, 7, 7
Row 2: 9, 9, 5, 5
Row 3: 6, 6, 8, 8

Page 159
Fast Facts 73
Row 1: 4, 5
Row 2: 7, 9
Row 3: 8, 7
Row 4: 9, 4, 6
Row 5: 8, 5, 6
Fast Facts 74
Row 1: 6, 7
Row 2: 5, 9
Row 3: 8, 6
Row 4: 9, 4, 5
Row 5: 4, 8, 7

Page 162
A. 9, 3, 6, 10, 7, 10
B. 6, 2, 5, 7, 6, 9
C. 9, 4, 10, 7, 7, 6
D. 4, 8, 6, 8, 9, 8
E. 2, 9, 9, 4, 10, 5
F. 8, 9, 9, 5, 10, 3

Page 163
A. 8, 10, 10, 4, 4, 9
B. 6, 6, 10, 9, 7, 4
C. 9, 10, 6, 8, 5, 10
D. 8, 3, 9, 10, 3, 9
E. 7, 9, 8, 2, 5, 9
F. 7, 1, 5, 9, 6, 7

Page 164
Row 1: 6, 5, 6, 8, 8
Row 2: 7, 6, 7, 8
Row 3: 7, 4, 7
Row 4: 5, 4, 5
Row 5: 8, 5, 8

Page 165
Fast Facts 75
Row 1: 8, 8
Row 2: 7, 5
Row 3: 6, 7
Row 4: 7, 8, 7
Row 5: 8, 8, 6
Fast Facts 76
Row 1: 8. 7
Row 2: 8, 7
Row 3: 8, 8
Row 4: 5, 7, 5
Row 5: 8, 7, 6

Page 168
A. 6, 5, 8, 9, 6, 8
B. 7, 8, 7, 7, 5, 6
C. 5, 7, 4, 7, 8, 9
D. 3, 7, 8, 9, 6, 6
E. 8, 9, 8, 7, 8, 6
F. 4, 5, 5, 9, 5, 8

Page 169
A. 9, 8, 10, 5, 4, 10
B. 9, 8, 7, 8, 8, 10
C. 6, 3, 7, 9, 8, 7
D. 5, 7, 6, 4, 7, 4
E. 8, 9, 5, 7, 6, 3
F. 8, 2, 6, 9, 10, 8

Page 170
A. 8, 7, 8, 10, 3
B. 5, 10, 5, 9, 5
C. 10, 7, 9, 8, 4
D. 8, 3, 2, 6, 6
E. 6, 9, 10, 8, 8
F. 10, 4, 7, 9, 7
G. 4, 8, 2, 5, 9
H. 8, 10, 9, 6, 6
I. 9, 3, 7, 6, 10
J. 5, 9, 10, 4, 7

Page 171
A. 9, 10, 5, 9, 7
B. 10, 6, 7, 1, 8
C. 10, 7, 9, 8, 6
D. 3, 6, 10, 6, 9
E. 5, 7, 9, 8, 7
F. 4, 9, 2, 10, 8
G. 8, 10, 5, 4, 8
H. 9, 4, 3, 8, 7
I. 6, 10, 4, 3, 9
J. 5, 7, 5, 10, 9

Correlations to NCTM Standards

Fact Mastery: Addition & Subtraction supports the National Council of Teachers of Mathematics (NCTM) *Principles and Standards for School Mathematics* (2000).

The activities in this book support the following Number and Operations Standard Expectations for Grades Pre-K–2.

1. **Students count and recognize the number of objects in a set.**

   The partner games in this book require students to count, and several of the strategies for addition and subtraction introduced in the book require counting.

2. **Students understand the relative position and size of ordinal and cardinal numbers.**

   Several of the activities in *Fact Mastery: Addition & Subtraction* require students to compare the size of cardinal numbers.

3. **Students develop whole number sense and use numbers in flexible ways, including relating, composing, and decomposing them.**

   The strategies introduced in this book support this standard.

4. **Students understand the meanings of addition and subtraction of whole numbers and how the two operations relate to each other.**

   The various strategies for addition and subtraction introduced in this book support this standard.

5. **Students understand what happens when they add or subtract whole numbers.**

   This book contains many addition and subtraction activities that support this standard.

6. **Students use a variety of strategies for whole-number computation, focusing on addition and subtraction.**

   This book introduces and reinforces many different addition and subtraction strategies, including counting on, switching addend order, doubles, doubles less one, doubles plus one, counting back, and thinking addition and using double facts and sums of 10.

7. **Students become fluent in basic number combinations for addition and subtraction.**

   All of the activities in *Fact Mastery: Addition & Subtraction* have the ultimate goal of developing fluency in addition and subtraction facts, so they all support this standard.

8. **Students use different methods and tools to compute, including concrete objects, mental math, estimation, and paper and pencil.**

   Students use mental math, concrete objects, and pencil and paper to do the activities in this book.

The activities in this book support the following Algebra Standard Expectations for Grades Pre-K–2:

1. **Students use objects, pictures, and symbols to model situations that involve the addition and subtraction of whole numbers.**

   In the "Show and Solve" activities in this book, students use math counters to model problems. On the "Think and Solve" pages, number lines are used to check answers.

The activities in this book support the following Number and Operations Standard Expectations for Grades 3–5:

1. **Students recognize equivalent ways to represent the same number and generate equivalent numbers by composing or decomposing.**

   Several of the activities in this book support this standard.

2. **Students understand and use properties of operations, such as the distributive property of multiplication over addition.**

   One of the addition strategies introduced in *Fact Mastery: Addition & Subtraction*, "Switching Order of Addends," uses the commutative property of addition.

3. **Students become fluent in adding, subtracting, multiplying, and dividing whole numbers.**

   The activities in this book support students in becoming fluent in addition and subtraction.

4. **Students select appropriate computation methods and tools from among mental math, estimation, and paper and pencil according to the context, and then use the selected methods and tools.**

   The various strategies and methods introduced in this book support this standard.